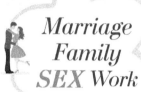

Marriage
Family
SEX *Work*

Your Life
in
HEAVEN

TRINITY ROYAL

YOUR LIFE IN HEAVEN

MARRIAGE, FAMILY, SEX, WORK, RELATIONSHIPS IN HEAVEN

TRINITY ROYAL

Library of Congress Control Number: 2023917894 | Digital ISBN: 978-1-957681-27-6

CONTENTS

Free books to our readers

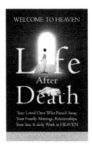

War in Heaven came to Earth. Satan Rebellion:

https://dl.bookfunnel.com/ea12ys3dmk

Your Life in Heaven:

https://dl.bookfunnel.com/vg451qpuzs

"No eye has seen, no ear has heard, and no mind has imagined what God has prepared for those who love him." – 1 Corinthians 2:9

INTRODUCTION

The idea of the deceased in Heaven enjoying eternal life can bring enormous comfort to the bereaved as well as hope to those who are suffering or facing dying. This has been the saving grace for many people throughout civilizations. It gives purpose to the challenging earthbound existence and lifts our hopes to tell us there is a beautiful end in sight and a reason for it all.

The pearly gates that will welcome us at the end of our life will receive us with open arms and we will enter the Kingdom of Eternal Salvation. That is what we are told anyway. It certainly makes getting through each day, and especially difficult days, that much easier.

The modern world creates constant stimulation that engages our senses through social media, television, and our electronic devices. It is easy to spend each day with the incessant noise and pulse of daily life amid that multitude of tasks that occupy our habits. You may begin to wonder, where does the room for connecting with the Divine fit in?

Without setting the time aside for intentional seeking of an internal connection with the great "One" in the sky, there is little room to allow for His presence to be in our lives. Some of us may try to carve out time to seek divinity and spiritual salvation through intellectual prowess by reading books. For example, the Bible and other spiritual resources provide sacred fuel while other people can simply fall prey to life's immediate pleasures that fulfill a void they may be feeling inside.

"There are over two billion Christians in the world, the vast majority of whom believe in heaven and hell. You die and your soul goes either to everlasting bliss or torment—or purgatory en route. 72% believe in a literal heaven" (Ehrman, 2020).

Before we begin, I must make clear who this book is for, and who it is not for, and what you may gain from it.

Who this book is for and who this book is NOT for

First and foremost, this book will talk about your and my life in Heaven. For the many believers of this Eternal Kingdom, what do we really know about it?

The idea of Heaven is well-known, and most people have a general idea of what it entails. But even Christ did not give many details about what Heaven exactly is. However, there are clues scattered in the Bible. We will put on the hat of a detective and explore.

The topics discussed here are very sensitive and every single one of us has opinions on these topics. Our opinions are formed by our upbringing or religious gatherings or teachings or from our mind filters based on life experiences. The same Bible verses can be interpreted in different ways by different people.

This book could challenge some of your preconceived notions.

Despite these challenges, I have still decided to attempt to share the knowledge and wisdom from my experience over the last two decades working with Christ and Heaven.

What this book is NOT:

- This book is NOT for people who do not believe in the existence of Heaven or Heavenly worlds.

- This book is NOT fiction or fantasy! While I do not claim to know everything about life in heaven, it is based on many years of painstaking research, as well as personal experiences.

- This book is NOT for atheists or those who do not believe they have a greater place within the workings of the universe.

- This book is not for closed-minded people who have made up their minds no matter what, and just want to find faults in everything else; you will miss the big picture. In all humbleness, this book may not be for you. My apologies

- Not all the info in this book is from the Holy Bible. So, if you think everything not in the Bible is blasphemy, this book may not be for you. I do apologize.

So, who is this book for?

- For those who are just too curious and want to know what Heaven is like

- For those who want to get a general idea of life in Heaven

- For those who want to know if Marriage and Relationships exist in Heaven

- For those who want to know if sexual intercourse exists in Heaven

- For those who want to know about life after mortal death

- For those who want to know what happened to loved ones after their mortal death

- For those who want to know what exactly happens to the soul, and spirit after death. Aren't these just new-age mumbo-jumbo concepts?

- For those who are curious about simple things like food or bathrooms in Heaven

- For those who want to know the time and space structure and levels in Heaven

- For those who think Heaven is a place of long eternal worship, a boring place and nothing to do.

- For those who want to know a bit deeper about the creator of the universe Jesus Christ

- People who are confused about life and not able to contemplate God's infinite creation.

- For those who just want to know the big picture of the meaning of life

If you are a member of one of the latter groups, prepare yourself.....this might just change your life.

What to Expect from This Book

This is book 2 of the series "Welcome to Heaven". In book 1 we have covered the foundational concepts. In this book, we will briefly discuss those foundational concepts and then build on them. The topics discussed in book 1 include:

- *Does Heaven exist? Isn't it just a mind concept? Is there biblical evidence?*

- Why do I even bother about Heaven? What is in it for me?

- What are the minimum requirements to go to Heaven or the ticket booth to Heaven?

- Why life on Earth is our kindergarten school?

- What body will you have in heaven?

- What happens to all our life experiences, including successes, failures, shortcomings, and illnesses after death?

- Why life on Earth is so difficult? Why is God/Christ not waving a magic wand and resolving all problems?

- And so much more..

For those who believe in Heaven, the inquiries and unanswered questions of *what life in Heaven looks like?*

don't necessarily keep most people awake at night, but the wonder of what Heaven really is all about does present itself as a curious phenomenon in the foundations of our lives. In fact, some people believe the deeper down the path of knowledge we go, the more we don't know and this makes understanding Heaven more curious.

This is a common adage— "the more we learn, the less we know"—and though it may be very true across a broad range of subjects, within the realm of knowing what there's to know about Heaven, we can deduce the clues.

For the truth-seekers and passionate mystics, these questions may induce states of existential uncertainty and restless unknowing, but rest assured, all of Creation is in the hands of the Almighty Creator and that also includes our doubts. What exactly are we Human beings made of other than flesh and bones?

The purpose of writing this book is to bring Heaven more real and bring it a bit closer to you. My hope is that those who are seeking to acquire knowledge to either create a new faith or empower their existing devotion to embrace God, the One Infinite Creator who abides in Heaven and brings Him closer in our daily lives.

Roadmap

In the first five chapters, we will cover some basics about heaven and the unseen parts of us that make us who we are. With the basics covered, we are ready to tackle the questions related to marriage, relationships, families, and sex in heaven.

Chapter One, we will explore what the Bible says about life on Earth in general, and how short it is compared to eternal life.

Chapter Two, we will explore different ways one can interact with heaven while still living in physical bodies. We will analyze the three well-known methods.

Chapter Three, we will explore the structure of creation in general and different levels of existence, namely material, semi-material, and non-material. This might be a deep topic for those new to this material. I have discussed extensively in earlier books; we will only cover the highlights in this chapter.

Chapter Four, we will explore the unseen parts of us that make us who we are, namely spirit and soul. What exactly they are and what is the function of each one of them? Again, this is high-level info here. I have covered details in my earlier books (links at the end).

Chapter Five, we will try and piece together the structure of creation and how it mimics the levels of existence. You may find one-to-one mapping. This could be an intriguing observation.

Chapter Six, now with the basics covered in the last few chapters, we are not ready to tackle the question about life in Heaven. We will explicitly talk about how beings in heaven communicate, what work they do, and what can you expect once you get there.

Chapter Seven, we will talk about your heavenly body. There are two different body forms generally speaking. We will cover what they are and their characteristics. Also, we will explore food the body needs and if bathrooms exist in heaven

Chapter Eight, we will explicitly talk about families, relationships, and marriage. Do you have family in heaven, do your loved ones know you, do they care for you, how different they are compared to your Earthly family? This is deep and interesting, do not miss this.

Chapter Nine, we will explore what Christ said about Marriages in heaven and if marriages exist in heaven.

Chapter Ten, we will talk about what most (actually all) avoid. Is there sexual intercourse in heaven? I will not spoil it by spilling the info. You definitely do not want to miss this. The answer could be much different than what you expect.

You are ready as you will ever be, let's open the doors of our minds and that of Heaven. Welcome to Heaven.

LIFE IS A VAPOR THAT VANISHES AT DAWN

In the New Testament Epistle from James, Jesus' brother, James writes in chapter 4, verses 14 and 15:

> Whereas ye know not what shall be on the morrow. For what is your life? It is even a vapour, that appeareth for a little time, and then vanishes away. For that ye ought to say, If the Lord will, we shall live, and do this, or that.

Many early Christians had the same kinds of questions and problems that are familiar to us even today. People were spending their time worrying about building up their treasures, concerning themselves with the ways of this world, and getting lost in unimportant things that did not point to Christ or toward goodness and the purpose of having a fulfilling life on Earth.

James felt that it was necessary to remind people that all that is given to us is the opportunity to trust in God, and that the time in which we have to do that is rather a brief one. James compares human life to a vapor that appears briefly and then vanishes away. It is as true today as it was for the original audience that James was writing to.

The point in sharing this is to simply say, that even if you live to be 100, this is still just a blink of an eye in the consideration of the time that the universe has been in existence. Even more than that, it is literally immeasurable when you look at the scope of all eternity.

No one knows the day or the hour that they will be called back home to Heaven. Death sleep comes for us all and is something that we cannot control. Each moment of each day may be our last. Even babies and young children, unfortunately, die before they can experience much of life. Teenagers and young adults on the brink of discovering their life's purpose can be here one day and gone the next. Life expectancy may be longer now than it was in Jesus' day, but the truth is, that the randomness of death is just around the corner for each of us.

It is just as James writes. Life is short and it vanishes soon and without warning. No one knows which day will be their last, so we need to work on developing the breadth of our experience, which means making the most out of each day. We need to always remember this brevity and uncertainty, and the dangerous combination they provide. Doing so is the prescription to cure the common ailment of procrastination.

Too often, we put off doing something for tomorrow that we could do today. We think we will always have more time until we realize we do not. Why not make the most of the day so that the future can be known instead of relegated to mere chance? The better we plan for this day, the more enjoyable the next one will be.

None of us will be perfect, and that is okay. God does not ask for us to be perfect. God does, however, ask for our faith and our trust in Him, and if we work to strive to be better each day, then we have the opportunity to go deeper in our faith and trust in God. It doesn't matter if we are given 20 years or 100; each day is a chance to trust more in God than the day before.

Ultimately, it is inevitable. One day each one of us will pass from this life to the next. In light of this, there are scriptures, like in Ecclesiastes that invite us to eat, drink, and be merry, but whatever we do, may it all bring glory to our God. All of our actions should be for the glory of our Creator.

None of us did anything to bring ourselves into this life. Our parents brought us here, and our God created the conditions of living that made it possible. Our God gave us a soul when we made the choice to trust in Him and have faith. If we did nothing to bring about this existence, what makes us think that we are the center of the story? God is the center of the story. As 1 Corinthians 6:19-20 reads:

"Don't you realize that your body is the temple of the Holy Spirit, who lives in you and was given to you by God? You do not belong to yourself, for God bought you with a high price. So, you must honor God with your body.

No one knows the time when this world will come to an end. Many prophets have come and gone and made their predictions about the Day of Judgement. They have used false equations and have been impure in their intentions most of the time.

That being said, it is clear that the time for harvest is coming to Earth. Without knowing the exact date or time, it can still be abundantly apparent that the Earth is ripening and the time for harvest is soon. This is discussed elsewhere in greater detail, but for the purposes of this chapter, let us focus on the fact that life as a whole is short, and life on Earth is particularly fragile, as it may curtain at any time.

HOW TO VISIT HEAVEN WHILE IN PHYSICAL

T he journey to Heaven is something to look forward to and full of surprises. Some people want to connect with Heaven so much that they'll do anything in this life to get there. The number of spiritual schools and teachers who practice "The Art of Spiritual Connection" is wide and numerous. In this modern day, it seems everyone is looking for a piece of salvation. The increased number of books and diversity of teachings about spiritual matters can leave one overwhelmed with the notion that this life really isn't good enough. They teach that there are many ways to reach the pearly gates of Bliss that will bring you the salvation and peace you're yearning for. We know that something is good in Heaven. God and his Kingdom teach that Heaven is here on earth. Often, the quest and search for His beloved Kingdom before our precious time on this planet has ended calls to us, and some would do anything to know what that is in the here and now.

As these chapters have been exploring, the beautiful Kingdom of Heaven is rich in bounty and glory. We also know this because it was the Apostle Paul who acknowledges that he has been there and tells us so.

The Apostle Paul is the only apostle in the Bible with the account that he has been to Heaven. The great interest in Apostle Paul's testimony is that his explanation is with such great humility of his experience that we are only left to believe that it is true. He spoke with such sacred silence that he even claimed that it was not He but another who had the fortunate experience. In sharing his experience, it reminds us that not only is it difficult to fathom the entirety of Heaven from our human perspective, but that only in sincere humbleness can we talk about it.

The Apostle Paul claims, "I must go on boasting. Though there is nothing to be gained by it, I will go on to visions and revelations of the Lord. I know a man in Christ who, fourteen years ago, was caught up to the third Heaven — whether in the body or out of the body, I do not know, God knows. And I know that this man was caught up into paradise — whether in the body or out of the body I do not know, God knows — and he heard things that cannot be told, which man may not utter. On behalf of this man, I will boast, but on my own behalf I will not boast, except of my weaknesses" (English Standard Version, 1971,) Paul is talking about himself, even though he says, "I know a man . . ." because two verses later he says, "To keep me from becoming conceited because of the surpassing greatness of the revelations, a thorn was given me in the flesh" (English Standard Version, 1971,).

The secrets of Heaven that can't be told are the main idea we can gather from Apostle Paul's account. It's true that he himself was the one who had this extraordinary experience and shared it with others while recognizing the sin of arrogance.

Ways to Get to Heaven

It is a great honor to receive the teaching that the greatness of Heaven is not for one to feel conceit or arrogance, and even though curiosity is integral, humility is key when understanding the majestic Kingdom of God. We live in a material world, yet the unseen is always with us. When we climb through the levels of consciousness, perhaps we can get a glimpse of Heaven, as some people have claimed. This section will explore the non-intentional experiences and the sober attempts that have been made to get to Heaven and what we can expect to find when we cross the threshold of this mortal plane. What are the ways to traverse this earthly plane and experience the paradise beyond without actually staying there? There are three ways that we can transcend the material and experience the realm of spirit that beholds the Kingdom of Heaven: Near Death Experience (NDE), dreams, visions, and out-of-body experiences, and meditation techniques.

Near Death Experience (NDE)

The idea of death is not something that many people perceive as a precious experience in their hearts unless, of course, they become witness to something spectacular. As a Christian or a follower of the Bible, when we know that the Kingdom of Heaven is on the other side of our afterlife and is a destination that one may even be able to look forward to, some try to get there in advance. There have been some experiences of unplanned awakenings, with accounts from people who have had such moving and shocking experiences that would truly inspire you, called NDEs. NDEs are experiences that take you to Heaven before you actually plan to be there. They usually occur during a traumatic event that often, but not always, onsets near the brink of death. If a person has had an NDE, then the experience presented was not of choice or seeking but as an unexpected, momentary gateway to the other side. With this experience, the opportunity presented itself for a person to come back. It's only for their return that accounts have been given for an afterlife. The results are shocking and leave the remainder of us mortals stupefied at what has been discovered at times and relieved to know that there really is more out there past this mortal coil.

There are many accounts of people who have been on the "other side" and then come back with insight and experience about how things are. We have heard of the famous "white light" or the tunnel that leads you closer and closer there. Even though that sounds suspicious, it's enthralling. One thing is for sure, the other side is a lot different than where we are now. For one thing, many people speak of great love, freedom, and having fewer worries than we have here. Across the board of studies about NDEs, there are similar perceptions that occur after a return from the NDE. Many people who have had the experience of dying have come back and report similar stories of their miraculous near-death experiences, from everywhere around the world They have claimed to feel a sense of separation from the body, and with this comes other characteristics that include an experience of a life review or scenes of their lives flashing before their eyes. These common experiences described in their personal stories add up to the fact that there are several stages in an afterlife journey.

Many people experience the same phenomena and witness the same sensations. ", or related phenomena such as out-of-body experiences, tend to have a fundamental effect on attitudes to death and dying, previous research has shown. Many people who have been through NDEs come out with a decreased fear of death. Among the main features of NDEs are sensations of altered time perception, seeing scenes from the past or the future, feelings of joy and peace, a sense of unity with the world, feeling of separation from the physical body, and apparent encounters with mystical beings, deceased spirits or religious figures" (Georgiou, 2022). The commonality of the findings of this research and studies proves that what's on the other side waiting for us can challenge our current perceptions of time, reduce fear of death, and experience unfathomable emotions of love and unity we could scarcely access with our current consciousness. The research has shown that NDEs and out-of-body experiences shift the fundamental perspectives of people on their return and leave impressionable insight about the "other side."

While not all NDEs may be positive, in fact, without a doubt, some experiences may just be terrifying. For the purposes of this book, finding the evidence of those who have had access to some form of mystical and ethereal essence supports that Heaven is truly waiting for us. Another study, reports that 64% of NDEs experience are unearthly, beautiful, mystical light, and that it's interesting that NDErs who had a positive near-death experience talk about an incredible, other-worldly kind of unconditional love that comes from a Being of pure, bright light. Based on their reports, this Being of light is the source of the love and power they experience and emanates warmth, comfort, and peace" (God of Light & Love, n.d). If you've ever had strange experiences of intense emotions, spiritual encounters with mystical beings, or experiences on this mortal plane, then it wouldn't come as a surprise if these experiences happen and are even magnified and even real in the afterlife, as these accounts attest to. Certainly, if one were to encounter such a presence of unconditional love and oneness, death must appear as an illusion. To be present and witness to such beauty in new dimensions that resonate deeply with a soul would be an inspiration. One could only return to this life with a change of attitude and have a positive outlook when you have something so beautiful to look forward to. I imagine people would be inclined to live with an attitude of service to this unconditional love, to become one with its innate power that can touch us all, even more than the current followers of Christ experience on this earth now.

These NDEs are very interesting to hear about, but of course, to the scientific mind, there isn't any conclusive evidence that they're real. In fact, they only shared stories from the minds and experiences of people who have had them without any proof or facts that support them. This brings into question the validity of these experiences, and you can ask yourself with the deepest insight of your own inner knowing, do you believe their experiences are real? In fact, when you consider the power and symbolism of your own perceptions of your presence on earth and vision of the afterlife, maybe this really is possible. Your own dreams can help you to imagine another world on the "other side" because dreams tell us that an afterlife may not be so hard to believe after all. If you think about it, you experience another world when you fall asleep. You close your eyes every night and enter other levels of perceptions and dimensions that were not thought possible until you wake up and reflect upon them. Dreams are also states that you may not always want to enter, especially if they're not of the good kind, yet they are very much a part of the fabric of our reality that weaves messages, provides insight, and affects our daily lives.

Dreams/Visions and Out of Body Experiences

When we sleep, we enter a dream world filled with imagery, sights, sounds, and experiences that we may or may not like. Filled with favorable experiences that live out our wildest hopes and fantasies or, alternatively, our scariest nightmares, dreams are a part of our multidimensional reality that become so fully aware of when we wake up. For some people, having dreams is a vivid experience they have to deal with on a daily basis, while for others, dreams don't appear to influence them at all or, at least, aren't remembered. If there's one tool we can access in our consciousness to communicate with the unseen world, it's through the dream world. At the end of the day, we may or may not be able to control them, but when our conscious mind is not in the way, so much can take place that shows up in the visions of our dreams.

Similar to trying to explain our dreams upon waking, the lack of being able to put feelings into words parallels the indescribable experience of having a moment of deep insight or feeling connected to God. This can be of nocturnal visitations or daydreams when we're able to spend time in prayerful moments. Even in the breakout pauses of our day, we can find peace and solace in His presence. Feeling the presence of God doesn't happen through our conscious mind but passes as a feeling through us, an essence that transcends human thought and eliminates the requirement for a deliberate articulation to try and express. When we embrace these feelings and moments of closeness to the Heavenly Father, we experience feelings closer to unity that connect us. In the dream state, this, too, may be easier to reach because our conscious mind is out of the way. God and Spirit are able to reach out to us and communicate with us more easily and with fewer obstacles of thought gratification that we may rely on too much at times. The messages that come through in our dreams can give us guidance and answers.

In the Bible, there are many examples of dreams providing guidance and even warnings. Many theologians and researchers study the role dreams have played in the Bible and they believe that these dreams have served significant purposes. "Dreams recorded in Scripture, however, serve a wider purpose established by God. They were given by the Father and recorded by His children for the sake of the church body throughout time. Every prophecy, direction, or warning is relevant to Christians today (Lucey, 2020). According to the passages and parables in the Bible, dreams have changed the course of history and people's lives. Most significantly, dreams influenced the birth and life of Jesus Christ. One of the best examples of these is found in the Book of Numbers. It shares that dreams hold the true inspiration for the word of God, "Then the Lord said,

'Listen to my words. Suppose there is a prophet among you. I, the Lord, make myself known to them in visions. I speak to them in dreams'" (New International Version, 2011, Numbers. 12:6). God says He will speak in dreams and if that's really the case, I would certainly want to wake up and listen! Dreams are the mystifying experiences in our daily lives that can bridge the gap from the unseen into the seen. As the Lord has made clear in this passage, they are effective tools for divine communication and even intervention.

In the Book of Genesis, the important interpretations of dreams offer meaning to the symbolic intricacies of life. In the lives of Mary and Joseph, these resulted in interventions that were fully present. This is seen when Pharaoh's officials, who felt dejected after having dreams that would tell of their fate, spoke to Joseph. They foretold of inescapable events such as the baker's dream, which prophesied the man's own death. The officials spoke to Joseph and said, "'We both had dreams,' they answered, 'but there is no one to interpret them.' Then Joseph said to them, 'Do not interpretations belong to God? Tell me your dreams' (New International Version, 2011, Genesis. 40:8). Joseph then accurately and successfully interpreted the dreams revealing that this scripture in the Bible shares in the power of dreams as foretelling truth. Joseph interpreted Pharaoh's dream to mean that there would be seven years of plenty and seven years of famine (New International Version, 2011, Genesis. 41: 28-41). Joseph's gift put him in a powerful position to implement a plan to protect Egypt from famine and rescue his family from potential starvation. The dreams Joseph interpreted for Pharaoh were both directional and prophetic dreams, demonstrating a wider purpose God has when He shares His word through dreams.

In the Old Testament, God gave His people dreams or the ability to interpret dreams in order to protect them from danger and fulfill His purposes. These include providing warning and protection and playing a significant role in the life and even survival of Jesus Christ. While Joseph shares with us his successful dream interpretation of the Pharaoh's officials, it's also through dreams that God speaks directly to Joseph for the birth and protection of Jesus. The Book of Matthew reveals how Joseph himself received a powerful message when he was instructed to wed Mary through the vision and voice of a dream due to the fact that she conceived a child through the Holy Spirit. Joseph received heavenly instruction as "An angel of the Lord appeared to him in a dream and said, 'Joseph son of David, do not be afraid to take Mary home as your wife, because what is conceived in her is from the Holy Spirit'" (New International Version, 2011, Matthew. 1:20). Contrary to what most men would believe and do at the time, he had clear instructions to wed Mary and become father to this child. Little did he know that he was to birth the actual Son of God.

The power of dreams continued to influence the birth and survival of Jesus when Herod, who had heard of the Son of God being born and, who would have great influence, ordered all the babies to be murdered. The Magi were directed not to return to Herod with news of Jesus for, "having been warned in a dream not to go back to Herod, they returned to their country by another route" (New International Version, 2011, Matthew. 2:12). Consequently, Joseph and Mary escaped to Egypt to protect Jesus. "When the danger had passed for Jesus, Joseph, and Mary, an angel of the Lord appeared in a dream to Joseph in Egypt and said, 'Get up, take the child and his mother and go to the land of Israel, for those who were trying to take the child's life are dead'" (New International Version, 2011, Matthew. 2:19-20). These scriptures confirm and reveal that the miraculous birth and protection of Jesus Christ was through the dream world. Joseph had so rightly understood that dreams have power and are the tools of God that have meaning and truth, as revealed in Genesis. Imagine if Joseph would not have paid attention to his dream and escape to Egypt. What would have been the consequences? The theme and power of dreams play throughout several parts of the Bible and Jesus's life, and we can even listen to them for the prophecy in our own lives.

How much of our lives is a free choice, or how much is guided by what we receive in our dreamscapes? Our mind may even set limits believing that this may even be possible, and many scientists have tried to understand their meaning. "The scientific world has not yet come up with an answer to why we dream, "there's no universally accepted definition of dreaming. One fairly safe catch-all is 'all perceptions, thoughts, or emotions experienced during sleep" (Lucey, 2020). While we don't have answers to what dreams are, no matter how advanced our society evolves, one thing is for certain, anyone who wakes up from them or may have even received messages or visitations from loved ones knows they're real. Perhaps the nightmares of childhood have left an indelible mark on their power and the true influence they can hold in our lives. But how often have you woken up from a dream, and it shifted the way you perceived things and your way of life or confirmed a feeling you may have had?

There are stages in the states of consciousness where you can play a role in your own dreams. Unknown to many, there are different levels of maturity in dreams. For those who wish to explore the world of dreams, there's a potential to develop a state called lucid dreaming that involves interacting with and controlling the narratives that unfold in the dream state. In a basic sense, we humans just dream of whatever without trying to influence the narratives. On the other extreme of dreaming is being able to be in conscious control of things as they unfold in a dream state. Yet be aware the power of the conscious and subconscious is mighty. It's recommended to always seek the protection of Jesus Christ and the Father of Creation when accessing or designing dream states that can have a significant influence on your life and take time to study how this might actually affect your life and spiritual belief system if you embark on this endeavor.

Meditation Techniques

The goal of mediation varies for each person who participates in it. While the New Age philosophies and mindset movements indicate that meditation has various goals for seeking "enlightenment" or other states of mindful bliss that were summarized in an earlier chapter, can meditation lead us through the gates of Heaven and into the actual Kingdom of God? Eastern traditions are the primary pioneers of meditation techniques that have come to the West primarily over the last century. There are many great accounts of people performing superhuman healings and achieving other states of ecstasy through meditation.

Jesus Christ was a man himself who may have also practiced meditation to connect with and enter into union with God, and this idea, too, may be challenged by many. Christians also read the Bible and practice a form of meditation that is integrated into a form of prayer. This controversial topic can lead to inspiring debates about knowing the Kingdom within versus the Kingdom of God that needs to tread very carefully in the ocean of spiritual seekers.

The Eastern traditions that foster meditation practice boast plenty of rituals to experience paradisiacal states from within. Is it possible to experience Heaven through meditation in the same way? The answer to this question leads to much controversy in terms of what the actual state of Heaven is and defined by whom. Meditation can serve many purposes that foster states of wellness through breath awareness and management, as well as nervous system regulation that offers elevated states of wellness, stress control, and feelings of peace that don't go unnoticed. But being mindful of your intention and focus will indicate your path as you traverse the complex and immense world of your own consciousness.

Grounding on Earth

It's accurate to say that having NDE means we rely on the accounts of people who have traversed this dimension to reach the other side and not by choice or out of manipulation. Perhaps like the apostle Paul, these accounts happened to share in the news and knowledge that there is something waiting for us on the other side, yet able to comprehend through true humility. Even if humanity really understood and truly knew the magnificence of Heaven, would we really be ready for that knowledge? Accessing or manipulating the dream states and meditation are controversial elements of accessing Heaven through this realm and before our time. It may also only result in the fabrication of what Heaven really is, and it's something that we can't have access to on this earthly plane, even though we try. In fact, many critics rally against these "New Age" movements and lucid dreaming because we are manipulating God's work, and it's not for us mortals to try and control. Isn't there a famous adage, Curiosity killed the cat? If we're not meant to have these experiences, then they would not be in our realm of existence, and certainly, God wouldn't let them enter into our lives. It was the Apostle Paul who could only humbly share the miraculous experience of Heaven and all its glory, and maybe we too should just wait for this Holy Day of reckoning to sit in the Seat of Judgement on the right-hand side of the Father when we are rightly called. As tempting as these glimpses of Heaven are, some experiences are meant to be sacred and delivered to us at the right time, even if curiosity takes over and we want to know what life in Heaven looks like.

While NDEs, dreams, and meditation are ways that take you into the experience of Heaven and closer to divine union with God, the true way into Heaven is through following the teachings of Christ, the son of God. In this life, we are given by God and trust that in service to Him and His holy righteousness, our pathway into Heaven is secured. Though we may be curious and anxious to experience the

Heavenly Kingdom before our time, God knows when it's the moment for us. Living in grace on this earth means that we accept this and live in gratitude for the earthly life we have with all its trials and tribulations. God's timing is very, very different from what we might want in terms of our expectations. While our clocks tick and time passes and operates in a linear time frame, God does not have the sense of time that we do. As much as we would like to have things go our way at the exact time we would like, that means God would have to operate on our schedule, and wouldn't that be just so convenient? But God most certainly has His own agenda. Surely, everything that is promised to you will happen in God's timing.

THE LEVELS OF HEAVEN

Most of us have some concept of Heaven, even if it has been characteristically one formed by movies like *What Dreams May Come or The Lovely Bones,* or thinking it involves meeting as in the movie *Bruce Almighty.* Just as a movie requires a set direction and props, Heaven may just as well be similarly designed, but by one of the best designers, set directors, and make-up artists combined into One and by God Himself. It is created by "the One", the Father who brings all things into being. The many levels of Heaven are as deliberately designed as any stage or movie set and include an intentional structure and order to creation that has existed since the dawn of time. Most certainly when we come to understand that our very soul, spirit, and identity are equally quite remarkable, then it comes as no surprise that Heaven too is just as real and astounding a place as the rest of all creation. In this chapter, we will explore the basic physical structure of Heaven and the various levels this Kingdom possesses.

While we can dream and imagine the white puffy clouds as being pillows that tuck us into our angel feather beds at night, and eternal sunshine exists as our backdrop as we float through in the expansive blue sky each day, it's actually not like that! Rather, Heaven is an actual location and not a mind concept. As taught by Jesus, he said, "I go to prepare a place for you" (New International Version, 1973, John 14:2). This place, Heaven, as told by Jesus, is prepared and planned. This intentionality of Heaven can set us at ease. We tend to put God in a box and try to explain with our limited conscious understanding what things are all about when in reality, God determines all, and we are only human after all. Imagine and allow for the incredible graces of our Holy Father to plan and have a dwelling place for us and know this to be true. When we can do this, the concept of Heaven becomes easily understandable and grasped as a relatable place that is waiting for us. The Father is loving and He has prepared for you a multitude of worlds on which you will continue to accumulate experience. It is simply impossible to gather all of the experiences of your soul's destiny in just one world, and only the initial one at that. When you have the path of the whole of creation laid down before you, with limitless experiences and boundless worlds, there are eternal structures you will see that will amaze you along your journey.

The Structure of Heaven

While you may be a beginner or have many years of growing and expanding your spiritual foundations on your relationship journey with God the Father, you may already know that Heaven is a place with multiple locations. We have established that it is not one single place but that the number of locations is varied and even infinite. For some, this may be common knowledge, whereas for others, it may be a new concept. Regardless, bringing you the reader to this point of awareness and comprehension is key for this part of the book and for the remainder of the chapters as we will begin to traverse the physical structures of Heaven as well as our layers of consciousness to get there. Be sure to go slow and take time to explore, understand, and integrate the following concepts that support ideas relating to the structure of Heaven, especially if some of these ideas may be new to you.

We can classify the structure of reality and worlds as categorized as layers into 3 broad categories that range from the material world being the most-dense to non-material as the least dense. Then there is Paradise where God, the deity resides.

1. Material worlds (physical worlds like Earth)

2. Semi-material worlds (transition worlds, also called Soul or Morontia worlds)

3. Non-material worlds (Spirit Worlds)

4. Paradise (God's abode, beyond time and space)

The structure, makeup, and complexity of worlds increase as one moves from the lower to the higher dimensional levels not in physical complexity, but in their frequency. Imagine that each level corresponds with a dimension. The less dense we are in the material world, the higher the frequency in the less-dense dimension. And, the frequencies of higher dimensions are more complex than the one below. Let me explain this further. If we were to place living beings in the most dense material plane, it is easy to comprehend that the chemical composition and complexity of the level above is higher than the level below yet appears and is more physically dense. Higher levels or dimensions require less food or sustenance than a living being would consume but are more complex in frequency. Overall, it is therefore safe to assume that food or sustenance requirements will reduce as body-form frequencies increase.

Think of it in relation to the concept of vapor outlined in an earlier chapter that rises without having form or density. The higher you go, the higher the senses become and less sustenance is required. At some point, experiences beyond the five senses will start to open. This can lead to the understanding that the abilities that people have in the higher Heavens are more complex than what we are accustomed to and may be represented through advanced telepathy or having other super-sensory skills or powers that equate with being generally common for that level or dimension. Forget the internet, imagine how fast messages could arrive if they were simply sent and received on a mental signal that didn't require opening up your email and reading it, let alone finding the "on" switch. The four worlds are broken down individually and outlined below and will clarify the levels of dimensions and densities by which our human body, soul, and spirit can experience in one or more lifetimes.

The three worlds of time and space

Material world (Physical worlds like Earth)

The material world is right outside your doorstep. We are fully aware of this earthly plane that can be felt by the ground that we walk upon, the seasons that change in our geographical locations, and the tides of the water that rise and fall with each phase of the moon. Each part of our Earth and its sphere is made up of certain chemical elements, for example, periodic table elements that all have certain vibrational frequencies that are not only found within our bodies but also the planet as a whole. For those who are familiar with the Shuman resonance, it acknowledges that "each lightning burst creates electromagnetic waves that begin to circle around Earth, captured between Earth's surface and a boundary about 60 miles up. Some of the waves—if they have just the right wavelength—combine, increasing in strength, to create a repeating atmospheric heartbeat known as Schumann resonance" (Wilson, 2013). These incredible electromagnetic waves are present around us and keep us in the earth's container, grounded in physicality and energetic impulses that make up and define the material world. The Earth, as we know it, also contains physical and dense beings—we humans—that require food and sustenance for our bodies. It is the food that we consume that fuels our own living energy and keeps our cellular structure, blood flow, and heartbeat alive, all maintained within the unique properties of this material dimension.

Semi-material worlds (Transition worlds also called Morontial worlds)

While Earth is a planet with a density we are certainly familiar with where we can walk, drive, and even fly in an airplane as part of our experience, what are the semi-material or transition worlds? *Morontia* is a term that refers to the vast level suspended between the material and the spiritual planes. Some textbooks specify there can be as many as seven worlds in this level. Each *Morontia* world is characteristically more refined, complex, and considerably less-dense than the one below it. While knowledge or even awareness of these worlds is not very common or well-known to most people, they are documented in the Bible.

One of Jesus' own disciples wrote about an 'enduring substance' of Heaven that can lead one to contemplate the existence of the *morontial* worlds, as it is written in Hebrews; "For ye had compassion of me in my bonds, and took joyfully the spoiling of your goods, knowing in yourselves that ye have in heaven a better and an enduring substance." (*King James Bible*, 2017/1769, Hebrews 10:34). As you rise in these semi-material worlds, they become less dense and, according to this biblical reference, existence has a more timeless frequency that may be best measured and described as immortality. Once we begin to transcend the earthly realm, vibrational frequencies increase and the spaces contain beings who are less dense and whose bodies need less food and sustenance for survival.

While it may be strange to think of beings other than humans who live in other dimensions and these angelic or other beings of reference are new to you, these beings living here have a body form technically called *Soul Body*. When Christ was resurrected, Christ's body was a *Soul Body* form. This is semi-material. If it was not, doubting Thomas would not have been able to touch the wounds of Jesus Christ whose biblical story demonstrates the importance of believing and having faith; "then he said to Thomas, 'Put your finger here, and see my hands; and put out your hand, and place it in my side. Do not disbelieve, but believe.' Thomas answered him, 'My Lord and my God!' Jesus said to him, 'Have you believed because you have seen me? Blessed are those who have not seen and yet have believed" (*New International Version*, 1973,). Not only does this story represent the power of faith during the time of Jesus' resurrection, but that the form of Jesus' body was a *Soul Body*. If His body was fully spirit, He would not have a form to be recognized by the apostles during His resurrection. Many did not recognize Him at first glance, unless He revealed Himself, meaning He did not have a pure physical body. When we begin to imagine the spaces beyond our physical and material world and the impermanence of our life and our own physical body, it clarifies how incredible our own human body is and the fact that a *Soul Body* and other creatures exist is entirely fathomable. Perhaps it is when we acknowledge the spiritual world and complete transcendence that many begin to scratch their heads and wonder if spiritual ascension is feasible. This semi-material world may introduce some notions of *Soul Body* and impermanence, but it is the spirit worlds that take us to yet a higher frequency even more astounding.

Spirit Worlds (Non-material)

The spirit worlds might be easier to imagine if you have spent time watching science fiction movies of mythical realms and creatures that walk on other planets. While you witness and experience the visuals of these places through colorfully filmed productions, the spiritual world, distinct from the physical world, can be perceived just as incredible. But true depictions of the spiritual world may not be entirely possible due to subjective realities and our lack of ability to perceive them. I will do my best here to describe these spaces of the spiritual world that may not elude all of us. According to the best of my knowledge and experience, there are numerous spirit worlds. As we can best imagine they are different from the material world grounded in earth. The spirit worlds have energy wavelengths and celestial bodies that require food and substance yet at a much lesser frequency. The spirit is 100% light and therefore there is no substance to the body form. There is no need for food or sustenance for the celestial beings that are 100% light because the spirit is self-generating. It is possible that many beings who are from spirit worlds came to Earth as planetary teachers and are walking among us.

If you can imagine the spirit as light, then it is possible to comprehend that the vibrations of a spirit being is very high, meaning that their frequency operates not on the dense emotions of fear, hate, or sorrow as an example, but contains more love, joy, and gratitude. Aside from the amount of information that we can find on the internet these days, presently and historically we have seen pictures of these celestial beings with halos around their heads, like those of Christ, and maybe even floating above in the air. I believe this represents a self-generating glow of Spirit. This representation of divinity or beings of divine stature are celestial beings who live in the spirit worlds that surround us and exist on different dimensions. The spirit world is a level that is one dimension lower than Heaven or, for all intents and purposes, what may also be referred to as Paradise in this part of the book.

Paradise

The best possible attempt to describe and define God's abode and utilize the most appropriate English word possible would be *Paradise*. This place isn't referring to the five-star hotel situated on the turquoise oceanfront property of a tropical island that we may dream about but, if you set your imagination on a place that is uniquely unfathomable to our limited consciousness, you might just be able to comprehend it. Why is the word "Paradise" appropriate to refer to Heaven? When understanding the origin of the word Paradise from early English, French, and Latin, it has interestingly enough been directly translated as 'The Garden of Eden' (Etymonline, 2022). This makes this choice of word quite appropriate, it appears, as it relates to the book of Genesis as one of the first Books in the Bible. The Garden of Eden "is the story of the heavens and the Earth when they were made, in the day the Lord God made the Earth and the heavens" (*New International Version*, 1973, Genesis 2:4-6). Paradise is used frequently throughout the Bible including the book of Luke when it says, "and Jesus said unto him. Verily I say unto thee, Today shalt thou be with me in paradise" (*New International Version*, 1973,). Paradise is the dwelling place of the Trinity—God the Father, God the Eternal Son, and

God the Infinite Spirit—and conjures many ideal qualities to define the Heavenly Kingdom.

Paradise is the indwelling place of all beings and is where God himself resides in the Kingdom of all eternity. When a person dies, the soul and, as we addressed in earlier chapters, the spirit detaches and goes to Paradise to be in the presence of God. If we can suspend the limitations of our human consciousness momentarily, we may be able to grasp the infinite concept of this resurrected place referred to as Paradise. We can identify it as a place that has no time and exists in one eternal moment. Since everything created has movement, for example, the planets, stars, sun, and galaxies that are in constant motion and so in tune with the expansiveness of the universe and unequivocal harmony, there is another end of the spectrum. It is possible to imagine that no time or space can exist either. Can you imagine it? Can you resonate with both perspectives of the duality of the existence within our universe created by God? Is it possible to comprehend or exist in absolute movement and utter stillness while being in a timeless place where God exists in all realms with an eternal presence? Many do believe this is possible.

WHAT ARE WE MADE OF OTHER THAN FLESH AND BLOOD?

We are unique and individual beings created in God's likeness and all attuned with an individual life essence.

We are composed of physical and non-physical parts whose existence has been attempted to be proven in religions across the world. For some, the desire for this connection with the non-physical parts of ourselves has driven people to develop their relationship and divine union with God, the Father by which soul and spirit become identifiable and integrated with our identity. Before delving into an exploration of the soul and spirit, let's first take a look at the identity that is most familiar and more commonly perceptible to us.

We live in our bodies our whole lives. If we take the time and focus to connect, we can feel deep within us there is something that transcends physical nature. While we can't quite grasp or touch what it really is, we have a sense of something non-physical being present within us.

This subtle presence is what people call by different names including Soul, Spirit, Atman, God, Higher-self, and Chi..Etc... Depending on your evolutionary journey with God, it may be easily experienced and intuitively observed.

Let's spend some time knowing the basics, and the fundamentals of these non-physical things that play a major role in our existence.

God's Spirit with-in

Each person is endowed with the divine spark of life from the Creator God that provides and sustains life in a physical material body. This divine spark residing inside of you is your Spirit. The fragment of God Himself, which is bestowed to each person in all glory of uniqueness and delight, can be referred to as spirit.

Then the LORD God formed a man from the dust of the ground and breathed into his nostrils the breath of life, and the man became a living being - Genesis 2:7

The spirit is God's indwelling presence within this spark and is always connected to Him. The spirit is known by many names across spiritual teachings, including but not limited to.... The Higher Self, the Indwelling Spirit, the Over-soul, the Ka, God Fragment, the Thought Adjuster, and many others. While these terms are expansive and represent different elements of our perceptions and ways of understanding God, the main idea is that the spirit seeks its expression in the lives of its indwelling hosts, or in other words, us humans. When this expression of spirit is manifested, it creates the connection of God within the non-physical element of every human who embraces their spirit, thereby supporting the notion that we are all "One."

"You are made in the image of God" (Genesis 1:26-27).

The Spirit of God within is pure and clean as God and just as perfect and pristine as it was when God gifted it to us at our birth. This bestowed divine spirit indwells in you, patiently waiting until you are ready to acknowledge and start to work together. One of the main teachings of Christ on Earth was to awaken humans to this divine presence within. The more you explore your Inner Kingdom, the more God is revealed to you.

That which is eternal is required

The physical self is, however, easily polluted. Our thoughts and actions and the way that we neglect our physical bodies take a toll over time and we are left with increasingly marred and imperfect bodies. To be clear, this is not a statement on people who may have different physical abilities. No one is "less than" because of needing a wheelchair any more than someone would be considered imperfect because they need glasses. No, this is specifically about defiling the body with impurities that, regardless of physical capabilities, will eventually happen to all human bodies. While the physical body can be so degraded, used up, and will ultimately experience death, the Spirit does not and cannot be polluted by our thoughts and actions. In fact, the Spirit, because it is of God, is just as pure and clean as God and just as perfect and pristine as it was when God gifted it to us at our birth.

Upon the death of the mortal physical body, your identity, and your personality will end here unless there is something that is beyond the material realm that can carry your experiences, your successes, and failures, all your good and bad experiences which gives you a character and unique personality. Only if there is such a thing that can exist after material demise, one can exist eternally.

I declare to you, brothers and sisters, that flesh and blood cannot inherit the kingdom of God, nor does the perishable inherit the imperishable. - 1 Corinthians 15:50

So if the spirit cannot carry your essence forward into eternal life, then there should be something else that is needed to carry your essence, your character, and your personality after death. This new essence is called the Soul. This is God's gift for eternal life.

Birth of a Soul

At about the age of four or five years old, more or less, the material mind starts to become mature enough to make moral choices. If you have children, or if you remember your early years, you know that this is about the time when enough learning has taken place that a child is beginning to listen, question, explore, and make decisions that can impact others greatly. Too much before five, and the child largely doesn't know any better.

There is the beginning of this new entity that will continue to grow with the child as it matures and ages into adolescence and young adulthood. This new thing comes about by being birthed of the material mind and the in-dwelling spirit that makes way for a new entity that is neither material nor non-material. It is instead, a semi-material matter known as the soul.

The mother of this new entity is the material mind, and the Father of this new entity is the non-material spirit. The semi-material nature that we popularly call the soul. Many books refer to this as Morontia as well.

This semi-material construct carries yourself, your personality, and your identity. Because we have the semi-material soul, we have the blending of the human (the personality of the material mind) and the Divine (the identity of the spirit) which gives the capacity for the self to experience life either as human or divine.

The choice as to how it goes about this liminal work is up to us. The soul gives us the potential as the intermediary between the physical and the nonphysical, between material human and non-material God, but only through our own intentional choices do we amplify the part of the soul that leans towards the Divine and away from our base, limited, and ultimately temporary physical selves. The soul is another selfless gift of the Divine. It comes from God and gives us the opportunity to become God-like while still living in our human bodies.

Just as each person is unique here on Earth (even identical twins have their own bodies and minds), a soul is the unique identifier of the person in Heaven. The soul is that part of you that is eternal. You would not be able to experience the eternal Heaven through your earthly body. It is not meant to last beyond the time apportioned to it on Earth, and thus it would be incapable of hosting your true self throughout all of eternity. Only a soul can do that, which is why it is essential to have faith so that the self has a vessel through which it can experience the eternal goodness of Heaven. 1 John 2:17 tells us the words of the apostle John who wrote, "And the world is passing away along with its desires, but whoever does the will of God abides forever." Only in choosing to have faith in God will you have the opportunity to abide forever.

All your experiences are stored in your soul and become part of the soul's DNA. Every thought, word, and deed has an impression. Everything is an energetic vibration and gets recorded in the soul-DNA and becomes a part of your identity. When God or Christ sees you, they see your soul as your identity. They do not see the physical appearance that you might identify yourself as. Transitory physical identification is an illusion in some ways, yet these combined components of your soul signature develop throughout your life as your soul's DNA evolves into your unique energetic expression.

Once you have a soul, you are an eternal being with a unique signature in all of creation. God and the angels will identify you with your soul signature. Your name and physical body no longer carry meaning. The truth is they never did. Those were only placeholders for your physical journey.

Jesus says, "For this is the will of My Father, that everyone who beholds the Son and believes in Him will have eternal life, and I Myself will raise him up on the last day."

Spirit is your identity

If there is no unique identity, then all Angels and Humans would think and act the same way every time and everywhere. This does not make sense. Identity of uniqueness is a gift from God to Creation. Every Angel or Human has a unique identity.

It is our identity that we may be most familiar with. It is a non-physical construct of our environment and experiences that is defined and reflected by our family, friends, jobs, and hobbies. Even the feelings and emotions we carry throughout our days make up our constitution and form our identity. It might also be defined as your personality, and with that in mind, we know that everybody most certainly has one!

This identity always remains intact as we progress on our evolutionary journey, and it is our identity and personality that is a gift endowed by God as our unique expression. This unique expression is what makes up our soul and defines us with this uniqueness in all of creation. Our transitory physical identification is an illusion, subject to withering away or falling off at any time. This may come as a great relief to some who complain about parts of themselves, they wish would change or were different.

It is when you realize it is all a gift from God, and how we manage this physical vessel and accompanying identity characteristics that we associate with is really up to us. All the experiences we have and engage in are part of our identity. Every thought, word, and deed has an impression on us and they are carried forth into the personality of who we truly are, which is impermeable. Your identity is preserved throughout your existence and is only carried forth when you make that crossover from the physical to the spiritual world.

But what makes identity unique? It is God's spirit within.

The spirit is a gift from God to you and me. Spirit resides in the seat of the mind. However, this divine spark does not get polluted by our experiences. Spirit stays divine irrespective of how good or bad the person is, or irrespective of one's experiences either in physical or in the Heavens.

This divine spark or God's spirit not only provides life but also gives each one of us a unique identity. This uniqueness is unfathomable to understand with our Human mind. Once you progress onto higher levels of Heaven (discussed in other books), you are recognized by your unique signature which is your in-dwelling Spirit.

When any Heavenly being visits you, they know you by your Heavenly identity. Your earthly name has no value, never did. The names that we give ourselves identify flesh and bones.

I declare to you, brothers and sisters, that flesh and blood cannot inherit the kingdom of God, nor does the perishable inherit the imperishable. - 1 Corinthians 15:50

Our physical name or associations that we have on Earth do not carry into Heaven. These disappear as soon as you go through death-sleep. Your eternal identity is provided by the in-dwelling spirit.

God pull vs Mortal pull

God's in-dwelling spirit has a few other functions as well. This divine spark of God executes a gentle pull towards Heaven, towards God. I call this God-pull. The Spirit gently encourages us to be God-like, as the Spirit in-dwelling is in His image. After all, like attracts like.

This spirit within is our communication with God. So, each of us has a direct connection to God. If you are alive, no matter what your experiences might be, you have a direct one-to-one connection with the Divine.

One other function, the in-dwelling spirit has is to carry an imprint of your Soul. This serves two purposes. During the resurrection process (discussed later), the spirit will find your soul and there is a 1 to 1 relationship. Secondly, when you graduate to higher heavenly realms, your soul will be fused with Spirit, so there is only spirit, when this occurs all your experiences from the birth of the soul are preserved within your spirit. We will discuss this also in later chapters.

The soul carries your personality

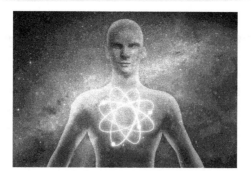

We have seen in the previous pages that the soul is a semi-material construct. It has its origins in the material mind (which is the mother) and divine spirit within (which is the Father). So the soul is both material and non-material at the same time.

If your soul identifies more with material nature, then the soul gravitates towards the material realm. However, if your soul chooses to do the will of Christ and believes in the existence of Heaven and eternal life, your soul's vibrations align with the Heavenly realm or the non-material realms.

However, most of us (including me) vacillate between these two opposite realms every day and perhaps all the time. It is just the nature of our Earthly existence and our living conditions.

When you look around at all the people you know and meet, it is incredible how different everyone is. Especially when it comes to all the colorful personalities. Personality is the characteristic given to us by God that deems our unique properties. We can easily identify a personality through various noticeable factors; for example, emotions such as optimism, pessimism, joy, sadness, light-heartedness, or seriousness. So when it comes to perceiving personality as unique it is obvious we are all unique.

The soul is an evolving construct just as our personality and character is. There is nothing static about a soul, just as there is nothing static to you and me. We change all the time whether growing or not-growing. We have plenty of experiences every day. What makes a soul unique is not only the template from when you were born but the experiences that happen on the journey through life that include emotional and mental imprinting.

The soul contains the sum of all your experiences throughout time and eternity in your life; your loves and losses; your victories and defeats; your trials and accomplishments, and so on and so on. It becomes your storyline. The choice of your soul landing in this physical body that comprises the embodied part of you holds the memories and development of your life. It can be said that the soul of man is an experiential acquisition, it is the self-reflective, truth-discerning, and spirit-perceiving part of humans whose constitution is solid yet remains permeable to the whimsical ups, downs, and ecstasies of life.

All your early and non-earthly experiences are stored in your soul and become part of the soul's DNA. Every thought, word, and deed has an impression. Everything is an energetic vibration that gets recorded in the DNA and becomes a part of your identity.

Thus, the Soul is the sum of all of our experiences, and conditioning, that makes up our personality.

The soul is semi-material and has substance to it

While the Spirit is one hundred percent light, the Soul is not. The soul is semi-material, meaning it has some substance to it. It has its origins in material-mind (which is the mother) and the Divine-spirit within (which is the Father). So soul is both material and non-material at the same time.

One physicist in the early 1900's tried to prove that our soul had weight. The experiment proved to be scientifically unsuccessful and there have been few to no documented studies of a similar nature. The study "attempted to measure the mass lost by a human when the soul departed the body. MacDougall attempted to measure the mass change of six patients at the moment of death. One of the six subjects lost three-quarters of an ounce (21.3 grams)" (21 *Grams Experiment*, 2022). The study has been referred to as the "The 21 Grams Experiment" because this was the weight lost by the patient and it was speculated that this difference could be attributed to the departure of the soul from the body.

STRUCTURE OF HEAVEN VS STRUCTURE OF HUMAN BEING

If you have paid close attention, we have seen that in a continuum space continuum of Creation has three broad categories namely material, semi-material, and non-material:

1. Material worlds (worlds like Earth)

2. Semi-material worlds (transition worlds, popularly known as Morontia worlds)

3. Non-material realms (Spirit realms)

Also, our Human being is comprised of:

1. Material body (physical body)

2. Semi-material (Soul resident in our material mind)

3. Non-material (God's Spirit within each of us)

A pattern begins to emerge. There is a correlation between material worlds (like Earth) to material bodies (physical bodies). Similarly, there is a co-relation between semi-material worlds and to semi-material part of us (Soul), like vise the Spirit part of us (Spirit with-in) to non-material worlds.

Fear of Death

Death happens to everything that lives. Some living things have short life spans. Some insects only live for a few weeks. Other living beings can live for hundreds of years. Some redwood trees have been living since before Christopher Columbus crossed the Atlantic Ocean. In the end though, death comes for us all. Typically, humans have a deep fear of death. There are an untold number of movies, books, and television shows that speak to the fear and avoidance of death. Of course, we hope that death can be as peaceful as possible, and we hope that all humans are able to live to old age and full lives. Unfortunately, we know that this is not always the case, however, and we have to be honest about the fact that death can come for any of us at any moment. So much of this fear comes from the fact that we don't talk enough and aren't comfortable with the understanding of what comes next.

In Western culture, at the very least, we are not often talking about death, funeral planning, or being comfortable with the idea of our death or the deaths of our loved ones. Hopefully in understanding this whole book, but this chapter specifically, we can begin the process of understanding better which will lower the fear that we have and increase our acceptance of the reality of death. This is not meant to be morbid, but hopefully helpful.

Many elderly people often come to a point in their lives when they feel ready for death and are accepting of it as an end to this life. If they've lived a good life and taken care of the gift of the soul that God has given them, then they can be assured that death is not the end. In the popular

Lord of the Rings books, the hobbit Pippin is sad about the death that seems to be certainly awaiting the forces of good when confronted by the forces of evil. The wise Gandalf replies to Pippin and says simply, but powerfully, "End? No. The journey does not end here. Death is just another path that we all must take." With this perspective, there is an acceptance of continuing on a path. It is up to us what happens on that path and where we go from here. We know now from previous chapters what we have to do in this life to ensure that death is not really the end, but is the continuation of the path for us.

When we truly appreciate what awaits us in death, it is no wonder that some people are very okay with, and even ready to die at the end of their lives. In Philippians 1:20-21, we read, "It is my eager expectation and hope that I will not be at all ashamed, but that with full courage now as always Christ will be honored in my body, whether by life or by death. For to me to live is Christ, and to die is gain."

What Happens at Death?

Now that we have the fundamentals of Heaven and the fundamental parts that make up a Human being, we are ready to tackle the question of what exactly happens at mortal death and also after death.

The physical body cannot exist in the eternal heavenly realms. It does not make sense to expect a body that is subject to the ravages of time, decay, and a general breakdown of itself, to be able to exist for eternity. If a sound body can only last 100 years here on Earth, it has no hope of carrying itself through to Heaven.

So will it be with the resurrection of the dead? The body that is sown is perishable, it is raised imperishable – 1 Corinthians 15:42

The body that a person who is graduating from Earth to Heaven will have is not going to be much like the body that is being held today. It won't look like a young version of yourself or be an expression of your body in its prime. That isn't how it works. The body will be totally different, but it also won't matter because the body won't carry with it all the value we place on our bodies today.

What happens to the Spirit after death?

Death is the absence of the breath-of-life or the absence of God's spirit with-in.

When a person dies, the in-dwelling Spark of God leaves the body and makes its way back to God from where it came. This is the most familiar thing for the Spirit. After all, the Spirit is from God is divine in nature, and knows its way back to God.

Christ on the cross said "Into your hand I commit my spirit" -Psalms 31:5. This shows that the Spirit knows how to get to the Father and is probably the only thing that the Spirit is aware of to do with no host.

What happens to the Soul after death?

Death is a word that can describe such finality. For this reason, books have often used the word death sleep. I have chosen to use this as well. The *death sleep* to refer to this period when our soul and spirit transition. The *death sleep* is the time of spiritual transformation and entrance into immortality and God's Kingdom of Heaven, "When the perishable has been clothed with the imperishable, and the mortal with immortality, then the saying that is written will come true: Death has been swallowed up in victory" (*New International Version*, 1973, 1 Corinthians 15:54).

This scripture claims that our mortal life does lead to immortality and the physical death is the separation of our body from our soul and spirit that is not covered in loss but celebrated in victory.

Do all souls go to Heaven? Of course not. I have discussed this extensively in book 1 of this series "Welcome to Heaven – Your Graduation from Kindergarten Earth to Heaven". I have a link at the end if you choose to read the same. I highly recommend it.

WHAT DOES LIFE IN HEAVEN LOOK LIKE?

U nderstanding Heaven and its welcoming doors doesn't take much when we gather all the facts around us and contemplate the Kingdom with a gracious heart. While we can sift through the passages of the Bible and attempt to frame this glorious place from our own limited human awareness and consciousness, gathering these pieces of understanding here with the main goal of analyzing and sharing in this wisdom is based on my understanding of the scriptures, research, and personal experiences.

There is enough knowledge to back up our understanding of Heaven and know what we can expect to experience. Even Christ did not give many details of what life in Heaven looks like, and this gave rise to a lot of speculation among theologians. If you're like me, and due to the number of questions and curiosity that leads you to consider yourself as "a heavenly brat" in a literal sense, try to give yourself a break. God understands the limitations of our human mind and the curiosity of knowledge it seeks.

Many years ago, when I was in the deep valleys of despair and I dived into an intense study of spiritual and religious matters, I heard God ask me if I needed some advice. Shockingly, yet not so surprisingly, I listened and knew it was the voice of God. At the time, I felt depressed and fed up with everything in life, and out of anger, I shouted in anger, "I don't want your advice. I want a Million dollars NOW!" God burst out laughing so loud, He knew it was my ego talking. Who said God does not have a sense of humor?

When speaking with God, you certainly aren't messing around with just anyone. Not only does this experience stick with me until this day, but it's also a reminder that God connects on a personal level, and loves humor and laughter. To this day, I'm still living and working a 9-5 job on a monthly paycheck. With this in mind and as you continue reading this chapter, it's most important to remember that God works in His own time and meets you at the level of your consciousness. God and Heavenly beings do not give in to your ego. If you can accept this, then I believe you may have come that little bit closer to accessing the secret elixir of life- it's essentially what's found in your heart and your relationship with God. This, combined with the knowledge that all of Heaven, including God, Christ, and the angels, love humor and want to laugh, sing, and dance and live life fully, abundantly, and worship the Creator with joy and not out of compulsion.

While you may consider the incessant questioning of the topic of Heaven annoys the best of the Angels within the Heavenly Kingdom, we have a right to postulate, speculate, and with the most fervent inquisition, imagine what the Heavenly Kingdom might be like in all of its glorious details. After all, if this is the place we are destined to go, it makes sense that we would like to know more about it. This chapter is for those who want to try and satisfy their curiosity about what awaits them in their daily life in the eternal Kingdom or at least in the first levels of Heaven. Regardless of this chapter's speculation, it is with an innocent heart I attempt to describe this place that holds so much wonder in our hearts, but without getting too caught up in the nitty-gritty details of Heaven and life. When we place our trust, hope, and faith in Christ, we know we are in good hands. Everything is in the proper place, and we'll arrive at the proper time.

Okay, we are in Heaven! Now What?

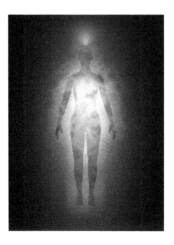

The mystery of God never ceases to amaze me. For those with abiding faith who trust and believe in the magnificence of the Father, our Creator, surely Heaven is not disappointing. We have been told that Heaven is worth it. There's eternal bliss, life is eternal, there's peace and joy, and there are countless Angels beyond our imaginations that make it worth living this earthly life and dying for. The Kingdom of Heaven is an eternal journey, and it's for the believers and seekers of righteousness that it awaits. As it is written, "What no eye has seen, nor ear heard, nor the heart of man imagined, what God has prepared for those who love him" (New International Version, 2011. 1 Corinthians. 2:9). However, we can't truly know this place without having faith and a love for the God who has created us. The burden of life can be pressing upon our earthly soul, but as we endure its lessons and the crosses that we have to carry in this life, Heaven will surely release us from these earthly bonds. It claims in Revelation, "He will wipe away every tear from their eyes, and death shall be no more, neither shall there be mourning, nor crying, nor pain anymore, for the former things have passed away" (English Standard Version, 1971 Revelation. 21:4) The gates of Heaven are waiting for us, and needless to say, there are many questions that can influence our perceptions and hope. This chapter seeks to explain some of them and attempt to answer the question, what does Heaven actually look like?

Communication

Living in paradise means that you will be with other souls in the Kingdom of Heaven. Certainly, joy and heavenly laughter exist when you get through those pearly gates, but needless to say, there will be a transition time required. In this process of transitory evolution, there will be a new way of thinking and being, including how you communicate. We may not need to have the latest iPhone or rely on GPS to get to go somewhere or connect with those we love in the heavenly realm. Communicating with Christ, God, and the Heavenly angels probably won't rely on text or Messenger services. Communication will be different than it ever has been known to you before. While our electronic devices are necessary and greatly appreciated in this mortal plane, when you pass through Heaven's doors, the new ways to understand and communicate with others will be at the next level too. This occurs upon the understanding and realization that your Soul body has many extra senses that will open up and evolve. You will have your own messenger services, and among them is telepathy, which is known as being able to read others' thoughts. I believe telepathy will be the general method of communication in Heaven. Also, being there at the right time and place may not be a random event anymore but something that happens frequently and without surprise. Because this is just how things operate on a daily basis in this Kingdom of God's Creation.

Your work in Heaven

In terms of work and making a living, some people predict that Heaven can be seen as a forever retirement home. Unlike Earth, there is no struggle to survive, and getting a 9-to-5 job to pay the mortgage is not something that will be a requirement for you. When we leave this mortal plane, we enter a dimension and a perpetual state of safety and security that only God's Kingdom can provide. Each being has all that is needed, including food, clothing, and shelter. While this may be difficult to imagine at this time in your life for some of you. All beings will be in service to one another and many levels to the Kingdom of Heaven, not only house choruses and multitudes of angels, of which you will be one, but you will be a part of His grand symphony and community of children.

What you will do on a daily basis is up to you. There are also angels whose sole purpose is to understand what your desires are and help you to find your passions or your desires. You will choose what you want to do, and no one can enforce anything on you. However, having a mindset based in goodness and righteousness also supports your state of consciousness that is focused on prayer and devotion to Christ and God the Father. This will neither be affected by distractions after a long day of hard work at your day job nor by watching the latest series of interesting on your cable network that may be a part of your daily routine here. You and God's angels will end up choosing that which is suitable for you and ready for you at any given moment.

The profession you choose depends on your Soul purpose, your skills, and your aspirations. No one will enforce what you must do. It can be considered as voluntary work that you enjoy doing and want to learn and contribute. The professions can be any in the realms of music, science, leadership positions, art, technology, spiritual teaching...etc. Heaven is much more dynamic and has more opportunities than Earth life presents. On Earth, most of us have a 9 to 5 job to pay for bills, to be able to put food on the table, and general family maintenance. In Heaven, all basics are met, and there is no struggle for survival.

Temples in Heaven

It may seem strange that once you get to Heaven, you'll still be praying. I mean, isn't that what life is on earth for? Once you get past those gates, you've made it, right? The heart and soul of a believer in God means that this eternal love and devotion never ceases. Heaven provides the perfect place for more devotional practice. As we know, Heaven houses many rooms, mansions, and people, the places of worship will be everywhere, and the practice of spirituality will still exist in Heaven. Many authors refer to these temples as Morontia temples and there are many.

All angels worship God and Christ, and when you get there, there won't be much difference. However, there are spiritual leaders, temples to visit, and schools of thought that teach about creation and different levels of Heaven, Christ, and God, while you're there. Here on earth, many people take pilgrimages to learn about God and become closer to Him. Likewise, in Heaven, the communities and people will all be focused on the same principles of worship, where spiritual closeness to divine oneness and evolution is often together or in groups where learning and growth are easily facilitated.

The Heavenly Community

It's when people gather in the community that we can share and delight in the teaching of Christ more profoundly. Knowing more people will be praying and celebrating Christ and the Kingdom of Heaven together, it's easy to imagine your arrival in the Heavenly community will indeed add to the fanfare. In previous chapters, we have addressed the multitude of people who will be there, and all of them bear differences yet possess the same devotion. The Bible also acknowledges that there is a "great multitude" of people who exist in Heaven. "After this, I looked, and behold a great multitude that no one could number, from every nation, from all tribes and peoples and languages, standing before the throne and before the Lamb, clothed in white robes, with palm branches in their hands" (New International Version, 2011,). To envision such a glorious uniting of world nations, without borders in the Kingdom of Heaven, is thrilling and sublime. Heaven will truly house the believers of the Creator of the world as One in peace and unity.

Money in Heaven

There is no monetary system in heaven. Your richness is not measured by your bank balance or your possessions. Sorry, Jeff Bezos, Bill Gates, Elon. Your true wealth is your Soul experiences, the richness of love, and the good intentions you carry. You will be your soul-like. The radiance you emit will display your inner glory. Similar to the barter system people exchange favors for each other, but there is no concept of money transactions.

Elements of Creation in Heaven

In our material world all of the things we see, feel or touch have a chemical composition that we have defined in our periodic table (118+ elements). Also, we have five senses touch, sight, hearing, smell, and taste. In heaven the number of elements is much more and more refined, the colors visible are so many more, and senses are not limited to those we know of. Much of this this explained well by the authors of Truthbook.

Pain and illness

There is no pain and illness in heaven. There is no pain on earth that heaven cannot heal.

> "He will wipe away every tear from their eyes, and death shall be no more, neither shall there be mourning, nor crying, nor pain anymore, for the former things have passed away" (Revelation 21:3-4).

YOUR NEW HEAVENLY BODY

The physical body cannot exist in the eternal heavenly realms. It does not make sense to expect a body that is subject to the ravages of time, decay, and a general breakdown of itself, to be able to exist for eternity. If a sound body can only last 100 years here on Earth, it has no hope of carrying itself through to Heaven.

The body that a person who is graduating from Earth to Heaven will have is not going to be much like the body that is being held today. It won't look like a young version of yourself or be an expression of your body in its prime. That isn't how it works. The body will be totally different, but it also won't matter because the body won't carry with it all the value, we place on our bodies today.

This is important because people who are differently abled physically or who have had trauma to their bodies will not carry that with them to the eternal realms. The body that you will have, should you be able to attain a soul, will be a combination of the soul, spirit, and a semi-transparent body. This is also called a soul-body or Morontia body. The combination of these parts of the body into one unified semi-transparent body is known as resurrection.

The resurrection that a person with a soul will have, is not about returning to Earth, however. There is no longer a need for this kindergarten experience. There is not an opportunity to repeat a grade. Instead, you are resurrected to this new body and a new way of experiencing your being. This body will be more suitable to the experience you are about to have in Heaven. Just as you need a submarine to take you to the bottom of the ocean instead of a car, a Morontia body will be the vessel that is most fitting for the heavenly travels that lay ahead of you.

The process of transition between these two forms is not immediate. Once a person graduates from earthly kindergarten to the first level in Heaven, that soul needs some time to acclimatize to this new level, having come from the earthly level below.

Just as a butterfly emerges from the caterpillar stage, so will the true personalities of human beings emerge on the heavenly world. There is more than just a bodily transition taking place during this time, too. During this grace period, which can last a few months, the soul is given permission to visit earthy loved ones. It is a form of closure, which is also important for the graduation ritual. In being able to conclude the time on Earth, the soul is freer to travel faithfully into the future realm.

Many people in our world today have shared experiences of having felt the presence of their loved ones for a short time after their physical death. You may know someone who has claimed to have seen the person walking in their familiar home, walking a route they used to walk, or even sleeping in their old bed. These sightings are not of the physical body but are an experience of this in-between state. After some time, again no more than just a few months, the soul then decides that it is ready to move on to continue to pursue the next lap of the journey.

Most certainly, when we transition from this life to the next, our physical vessel will be in an altered state. The moment of passing into Heaven means that our souls will shift into a new form that equals or may be referred to as semi-material bodies. Angels in Heaven have semi-material bodies or soul-form bodies that many theologians call "Glorious" bodies or Heavenly bodies. We know that once you are in Heaven, more of our Soul-like qualities will be revealed, meaning that our internal soul will be reflected more easily externally.

This new body can even be thought of as ethereal and existing of less density. While it's confusing to imagine that we will exist in a different body yet remain the same, scripture tells us that this is so. The Bible tells us that in Heaven, our offspring and name will remain (English Standard Version, 2001, Isaiah. 66:22). We will continue in the familiarity of our namesake and identity. Yet, considering we are born new, it makes sense that we receive a new name as well. The Bible advises and tells us that God is going to give us a new name that nobody else will know but us (English Standard Version, 2001, Revelations. 2:17).

Based on the wonderful lightness of your being and new soul form, it will take some getting used to, perhaps. However, there's nothing to fear, even though the unknown itself may be fearful. It's acknowledged in the scriptures of Corinthians that the new spiritual bodies will be incorruptible, glorious, beautiful, and powerful, "So also is the resurrection of the dead. It is sown in corruption; it is raised in corruption: it is sown in dishonor; it is raised in glory: it is sown in weakness; it is raised in power: it is sown a natural body; it is raised a spiritual body. There is a natural body, and there is a spiritual body" (King James Version, 1769, 1 Corinthians 15. 42-44). This new spiritual body will be yours. With your new heavenly body, you will also meet others who are in a similar reflection of you.

We'll know people more uniquely, as their authentic selves, and not live in an illusion that may feel so common in our earthly life. When you live with God, you are in service to God and not service to the Self, and as a result, all limits of illusion break free. In the Kingdom of Heaven, all beings are revealed as their authentic soul essence and in the true image and spirit of Christ and the Kingdom of God. Imagine the ability to live so openly and freely and to be able to foster relationships with others from such a sense of unity and oneness.

While it may be unsettling to imagine such transparency with others, imagine the freedom. There will be nothing to hide. Envision the innate authenticity of your soul and your highest essence on full display and light as a feather. Your vibrations, energy, and aura are seen by all and sensed by all, and there will be no judgment, just as you are able to do the same for all others. There will be no double standards, not be able to hide much, and it will be very much like a transparent book. Imagine an egoless existence free of the bonds that have dictated in your earthly life of how you should be based on your personality in this mortal life that holds limiting beliefs. These parts of you may have even been formed and developed from trauma, dysfunction, and distortion. When you enter the Heavenly realm, you are entering the Kingdom of God as His child, and you will be liberated of the heaviness that burdened you your whole life and housed your physical body.

Another helpful and useful way to understand this perspective of birthing into a new self is acknowledged by the Apostle Paul. Our original form, or identity, shall always be you, as your original identity. The Apostle Paul states to the Corinthians that a seed does not change until it is planted in the ground and "dies" first (New International Version, 2011, 1 Corinthians. 36). After a seed is planted, it sprouts and changes into something that's different in its composition and appearance from what it was before. We still, however, recognize that it came from the original source of a particular seed that was planted. Like any seed that sprouts from its original form, it grows into something new. This seed analogy expresses that our earthly physical bodies must first die and be 'sown' in the transference of life before it can change. The process of soul transference requires that the composition of our bodies change from flesh-based to spirit-based, yet we still remain the same.

The resurrected Christ had a Soul body form (or Morontia body). This body is neither materialistic or pure spirit, it is semi-material. This is why the disciples could not recognize Him unless He revealed Himself. Mary did not recognize Christ until Christ spoke. Disciples did not recognize until He revealed himself. Thomas did not believe unless he put his finger in the scars. There is much more to Christ's body and resurrection that is beyond the scope of this book. I do have a book dedicated to this topic if you are interested titled " What Happened on Easter Saturday?".

Our body in heaven will be similar to what Christ had on earth after resurrection.

Food and Drinks in Heaven

In your new Heavenly body, you will also enjoy the same things there, just as you did on Earth. You will be able to enjoy food and drink and share this with others. In the New Testament, the scripture is taken from the famous Last Supper as a symbolic moment to express the importance of food as well as support that our identities will remain unchanged in the Kingdom of God. While sharing the Passover meal with His disciples, Christ said, "Take this [cup] and divide it among yourselves; for I say to you, I will not drink of the fruit of the vine until the kingdom of God comes" (New American Standard Bible, 1995, Luke. 22:17-18). Christ promised that He and His disciples would drink the fruit of the vine together again in Heaven and acknowledged that the fruit of the vine shall be found in Heaven too. Even more uplifting is the notion of being gathered with many to enjoy the feasts and fruit of the vine together.

Jesus makes a similar but even more definite promise in the book of Matthew, "Many will come from east and west, and sit down with Abraham, Isaac, and Jacob in the kingdom of Heaven" (New American Standard Bible, 1995, Matthew. 8:11). As you will sit and enjoy feasting and sharing with others in the kingdom of Heaven, less food is required for your new semi-material for sustenance. Considerably much less than what is needed for the sustenance of your physical body here on this earth that loves to eat snacks at all hours of the day, myself included!

The amount of food intake depends on how much energy is needed for body sustenance. Recall that spirit body forms are pure light, so sustenance of food is needed. Spirit is self-generating that emanates light and energy from within itself.

However, soul bodies do require a minimal amount of food to sustain themselves as the body has some substance and shape to the form.

Food is required for body sustenance in the lower heaven, while there are no food requirements for higher-level spirits.

Bathrooms in Heaven

Your new glorified body of light, for the most part, vibrates at high frequencies. Eating dense food often makes the body denser and is not suitable for the body type that you will be transferring into once you pass the Heavenly gates. There is mention of food in the Bible that is freely available, found in nature, or as the "fruit of the vine." The amount of food needed to sustain the semi-material body is much less and will be of lighter origin. For example, scripture usually refers to the food or celebration that we consume as fruits. This food will be of pure origin and absorbed well by the body.

Imagine if there is bodily wastage that needs to be eliminated in Heaven and Paradise; Heaven will be smelly and become polluted. Will not be heaven anymore.

With this in mind, it's easy to say that there will be no waste that needs to be eliminated. Food will be available to all and in immaculate abundance. Imagine having what feels like a celebratory meal daily and enjoying a feast when you do eat. This will be an experience of not only food but in the fulfillment of your soul and shared with others who have all gathered in God's kingdom.

FAMILY LIFE IN THE HEAVENLY KINGDOM

The synopsis of what we can find in the Bible about marriage and families is a hot debate. Everyone has their own opinion and interprets the same Bible verses according to one's own spiritual growth and lens of experience. While one thing is certain, the nature of the afterlife and the Kingdom of Heaven is indeed a mystery that we can only do our best to try to comprehend with our mortal minds. This chapter provides an overlay of what Heaven means in terms of family and marriage.

Reading the following pages with an open mind will allow you to connect with your own inner knowledge too. Indeed, there are different interpretations on the matter of family and especially the union of souls, with some believing that there is marriage in Heaven and others holding the opinion that it doesn't exist.

If we hold the stance that there are no families in Heaven when you and I go to Heaven, we can envision that we'll eventually become lonely, self-centered, and maybe even introverted. If we try to think about it with our limited mindset, even though we worship God and Christ for a few hours a day, we may think it could start to become boring. Family in this life, for the most part, and ideologically, has taught us to have a connection, feel love, and be supported. Without this and a family in Heaven, it's easy to imagine that you will lack love and companionship.

It's said in the Book of Genesis, "It is not good for man to be alone" (English Standard Version, 2001, Genesis. 2:18). Almost everything of lasting value in civilization has its roots in the family. Without family, one may grow stoic and cold. Personal growth may even feel halted, and one may feel inclined not to offer up much in life as a possibility. A society that is able to flourish needs families. Throughout the history of ages, families have been the backbone of society. They share the blessings of culture and knowledge that flow from one generation to the next.

Heaven Is Made of Families

The Creator of the Universe Christ supports families and relationships

There is great importance given to Family and Relationships in Heavens. This is because our sovereign of the Universe Jesus Christ supports Family and relationships.

When a mortal being passes over to the other side after death, that being is allowed to return and visit the Family members who may be mourning the loss. It is common to see the deceased person in our dreams and visions a few days after death. I have personally experienced this with multiple family members (grandmother, grandfather, and uncles).

If the Universe of Christ did not give importance to Families, the person from the other side would not be allowed to visit. So, I am thankful to the Creator of our universe Jesus Christ for allowing the visitations of family members who have passed to the other side. It is also worth noting that the visits are not encouraged after some time, but just during the first few months, and then the frequency decreases. The beings who have passed on also have things they need to attend to.

There are so many personal stories and experiences of meeting deceased family members. I am certain most of us have these experiences. My paternal Uncle passed away late last year, and many of my family members have seen him multiple times in the first week of his passing away in his mortal body. This continued for many weeks. My aunt mentioned that my uncle was by her bedside all through the night when she was unwell, only to leave early morning.

The untimely death of my maternal uncle a few years ago, had all the family baffled by the manner of his death. No one knew the reason. Uncle himself came in a dream to his daughter and told her the details of what exactly happened that fateful day.

You can count on your heavenly family

Heaven is a thriving place full of dynamic nature, and we are all a welcome part of it. Being able to grow enough to get to Heaven is an achievement, and you are welcomed dearly. The angels and the kingdom of Heaven understand that Earth is a very hard place to graduate from. Families and, with the extension, Heavenly society will provide comfort, support, and guidance when you arrive there. You'll be able to count on your family in Heaven to welcome you with open arms. You have your Family in Heaven. How the family members are different from Earth's family is beyond the scope of discussion for this book.

Sharing one of my incidents many years ago, I was going through very dark valleys of life. I was processing so much on multiple levels that my body was unable to cope up. I felt like I was experiencing multiple physical micro deaths, and also had bad migraines that I recall telling the doctor that the pain is 9 out of 10. I did not how I was able to survive those days of loneliness. Later God told me that my family in Heaven was allowed to come and help out.

Family members on earth come in all shapes and sizes, good and ugly, friendly and unfriendly, loving and unloving..etc.. This is just the nature of life in limited consciousness. We do not get a choice to choose our Family members (at least for most of us), but there is some relation between the family we have on Earth vs that on Heaven. I am not very clear about all the details either, so will not attempt to explain.

You will recognize your heavenly family

The afterlife has held much mystery around the world and across cultures. It doesn't promise or come with guarantees, according to some, but with research and analysis of the scriptures, one thing is certain, heaven is a place where you'll meet with your loved ones again. There is every reason to believe that we will recognize and know our loved ones not only after our passing but for eternity. When you first arrive in Heaven, you can imagine that you will have plenty of angelic and family assistance during the first few weeks, wherein you spend time contemplating your earthly experiences.

Upon entering the gates of Heaven, don't be surprised if you see your loved one first. You will see those who have passed on before you, and you will recognize all of them. There may be more family members in Heaven than you are aware of on Earth. In the Old Testament, when a person died, the biblical writers said he was "gathered to his people" (New American Standard Bible, 1995, Genesis. 25:8; 35:29; 49:29; Numbers. 20:24; Judges. 2:10). While this imagery of being "gathered to your people" is truly inspiring and in addition to the Heavenly community who have housed your loved ones who have passed on, is really a dream come true to many.

In addition, you will have a continuing relationship with all those we knew on Earth and in Heaven. In Corinthians, the Apostle Paul declared: "For now we see in a mirror dimly, but then face to face. Now I know in part; then I shall know fully, even as I have been fully known" (English Standard Version, 2001, 1 Corinthians. 13:12). This scripture inspires and shares in the notion that "then, face to face," we'll see others that have known us as we see them. We're going to know our loved ones in Heaven and know each other plainly and clearly.

David in the Book of Samuel also acknowledges that his child will be waiting for him once he has left this earthly plane before him. When David's infant child died in the Book of 2 Samuel, David confidently said, "I shall go to him, but he shall not return to me" (New International Version, 2011, 2 Samuel. 12:23). When we pass on, we go to the gates of Heaven, from where we will not return to earth as David acknowledges. David evidently expected to see his child again and not just a nameless, faceless soul without an identity but that very child of his.

DOES MARRIAGE EXIST IN HEAVEN?

T hroughout the Bible, we know that pairing is the nature of God's creation. Every living species, including animals, pair to survive and live. A society with no pro-creation will likely die eventually. Survival of the human species, or any species for that matter, is dependent on pro-creation, and having children and creating a family has many advantages, as shared in Psalms, "No doubt about it: children are a gift from the Lord; the fruit of the womb is a divine reward" (New International Version, 2011, Psalm. 127:3-5). For those who have family, you may be reminded of the everlasting connection this brings and how you may gather in unity and hope. "Behold, how good and how pleasant it is For brethren to dwell together in unity" (King James Version, 1796, Psalm. 133:1). To imagine that God's Kingdom does not have families seems counterintuitive to all of His teachings based on righteousness.

On Earth, when two souls meet, and a bond is formed, marriage unites these two beings so that this bond lasts forever-this is family. It's viewed as a precious and esteemed relationship, even throughout many verses of the Bible.

But what happens to us in Heaven?

Do we get to form this bond with one another in matrimonial bliss and union? There's one verse in the Bible that all theologians refer to when discussing this topic that clearly states God's opinion on the matter. When speaking with one group of religious leaders, the Sadducees tried to trick Jesus with a question about marriage in Heaven. They didn't believe in the resurrection of the dead. Attempting to make him look foolish, they told Jesus of a woman who had seven husbands who all died. They asked him, "Now then, at the resurrection, whose wife will she be of the seven, since all of them were married to her?" (English Standard Version, 2001, Matthew. 22:28). Christ replied, "At the resurrection, people will neither marry nor be given in marriage; they will be like the angels in heaven" (English Standard Version, 2001, Matthew. 22:30).

This clearly states the view of scripture and confirms the absence of marital union when we enter those pearly gates. However, it does not negate the existence and the importance of Family and Relationships in Heaven

There are no marriages in Heaven. A being is not tied to another for any amount of time. There is complete freedom in heaven. There are no karmic issues or other factors that bind 2 people together. It is the choice of the two souls to come together to form a union according to their desires.

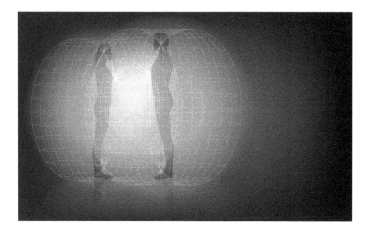

DOES SEXUAL INTERCOURSE EXIST IN HEAVEN?

Sex has been used for good and evil throughout the world and history since the dawn of time, and what a controversial topic it is. Considering it has such a powerful hold on some people or is completely revered by others, indeed, it's a significant part of our lives. We clearly need to approach what it says in the Bible and acknowledge that it has undoubtedly been a hotly debated topic among theologians for centuries.

Throughout various passages of the Bible, intercourse is supported among married couples and for the procreation of life. Practically speaking, for Kingdoms to exist, families are required. Yet the Bible does not refer to, or otherwise offer direct reference about, intercourse in Heaven. Only in the chapters of Leviticus will you find all the rules about how sex should not be used. Otherwise, and of importance here, let's refer to Genesis and other chapters where it says that besides expanding the human race, God designed intercourse for the physical, emotional, and spiritual union between one man and one woman for life (English Standard Version, 2001 Genesis. 2:18; 23–24; Matthew. 19:4–6; 1 Corinthians. 7:32–34).

In fact, further exploration reveals in Hebrews that God's design for sex between a married man and woman is good and honorable (English Standard Version, 2001, Hebrews. 13:4). While there are many distortions and perversions in all areas of society around the practices of sex, in the Bible, it is taught that there is nothing shameful, dirty, or dishonorable about it and it in fact, can be performed and reveal states of innocence, "the man and his wife were both naked, and they were not ashamed" (English Standard Version, 2001, Genesis. 2:25). The natural beauty and purpose of intercourse are supported throughout the Bible for man and woman in the union of marriage and to gracefully share in this beautiful experience.

In the animal world, sex is used only for the reproduction of the species. Animals do not usually engage in sex for purely pleasurable reasons; animals are not overly concerned with sex. It is purely instinctual.

But does sex exist in Heaven?

Theologians starkly differ, and all God-loving people have an opinion one way or another. It is a highly controversial topic. Without going into my personal experiences, I will give my opinion. Sex does exist in Heaven, but it is not exactly as our human minds conceive of sex on Earth. The word "union" is a better way to describe sex in heaven. Let's discuss further.

For Heaven to flourish, the existence is Families is necessary as families form the backbone of a structured society. For families to exist, procreation is required. Procreation can happen only with two opposite genders (male and female). There are both male and female angels. Both the energies of yin and yang are necessary and are ever present in all levels of heaven even unto paradise. Male and female are equal in the eyes of God, like a bird with two wings. In the words of the author of Truthbook, both male and female energies continue to fascinate each other in Heavens.

Just imagine having all females or all males in one family on Earth, it does not make sense to think about it. Does it make sense to have all males or all females in your Heavenly family?

The energies of passion are required for procreation, so it is in Heaven. Two souls of opposite genders choose each other and or are attracted to each other based on their soul's qualities and makeup. The difference between Earth and Heaven is that there are no double standards in Heaven, one cannot hide anything from other people, and everything is out and on full display in one's energy signature. You are your Soul-Like. There is no ego or lust associated with the union of two souls in heaven unlike that we experience on Earth.

The activity of procreation differs based on one's heavenly body. The soul-body form is semi-material in nature and has some substance to the body. There are the male and female reproductive organs. The spirit body form is non-material and has no form and there are no reproductive organs.

If there was no reproduction of any kind in Heaven, God would be the loneliest person ever. Every Angel high or low is a product of some sort of union between two beings. While I do not claim to know the details of the actual sexual process itself, I do know that sex in heaven is a union or joining of two souls or two spirits. This is done with great love for each other and devoid of ego and lust.

Procreation in Heaven is an act of tremendous joy minus ego and lust.

As above, so below

To most people, just going to Heaven is the end of all life mission. I agree it is the best thing and should be your only mission on Earth. I have discussed the minimum requirements to go to Heaven in Book 1, Welcome to Heaven. However, do you know Angles have to work to evolve themselves also, there is no end to growth and evolution in this infinite creation of our Creator.

Heaven is mysterious to many, but once you get to know it, you may be surprised to learn that life just flows naturally and does not feel very different from our life in limited consciousness. As above so below. It is only mysterious because one does not know it yet. Higher levels of heaven are more perfect...lower levels are not so. There is still duality and each of us has to grow and improve our worth to become a citizen of higher heavens. A big difference is the absence of darkness or Satan's hold on people.

CONCLUSION

E ach person reading this book has their perception of heaven. I have tried to give you a preview of my understanding of life in Heaven. However, I understand well some readers may not be on the same page. That is okay, we are all children of the most High and we have our belief patterns. I value your beliefs.

It is no surprise that the human mind likes to complicate matters. When it comes to Heaven and your relationship with God the Father, it is really quite simple: self-reflect and commune with the depths of Christ and the Creator within your heart. Contemplation of them in your mind, thoughts, and heart will then soon reflect in your outward life and it may not be so surprising how the presence of God will reveal Himself to you and eventually through you.

The Earth is the greatest 3D classroom there is. Whether you are aware of this and know that this is the great School of Life places you in learning conditions to reveal the states of your own Godhead of goodness. We are born on this great Earth with the spark of our Divine soul essence for unique and specific reasons. While living under the great law of the Divine, for those who seek higher levels of consciousness and devotion to be of service to the Almighty Father in the Kingdom of Heaven, the most difficult "pass" carries with it a great reward as well.

When you walk on this path, you may feel alone in some parts of the journey. You are never alone. When you are ready for the next step, your guidance arrives. This is a common process and while at times you may feel like you are a dry well with no ounce of water in sight except for the stinging tears that may drop from a sorrow-filled heart due to obstacles that may challenge the very essence of you who you are, these are the steps and stages that will lead you to the fountain of knowledge.

Christ will guide you to the eternal ocean of love and connection to a Kingdom that is, always has been, and will always be yours as a child of God. Each moment grants us the opportunity to receive lessons and inspiration in our evolutionary steps on this earthly plane and with the appreciation of our physical vessel that takes us through this journey. There truly is no end to the amount of growth and experiences that one can attain in Heaven.

Welcome to Heaven. You are worth it. Enjoy Your Life in heaven.

THANK YOU

I want to personally Thank you for reading this book.

I have poured my Heart and Soul into these pages. I hope you have gained some valuable insights from the information presented. Please consider leaving your valuable review. Your review and feedback are important to me. Thank you so much.

⭐ ⭐ ⭐ ⭐ ⭐

Scan to leave a Review:

BONUS CHAPTER: THE ADVANTAGES OF BEING ON EARTH

S ome of the greatest inventions and developments in the history of humanity have come about by people who have experienced extreme hardship. People who have lost parents at an early age are often more likely to thrive and catapult themselves into amazing positions later in life. Maybe they feel that they have nothing to lose. Maybe they feel that they have already lost so much that they wonder why not go for seemingly unattainable goals. What is most likely is that these people have been so honed by the difficult experiences in their early life that they are able to weather any storm that they may be forced to reckon with as they get older.

Think of how people train for marathons or build strength in their bodies. Marathon trainers have to endure long-distance runs that break down the limits of their bodies before they can build up new thresholds of capability. Bodybuilders also have to push their muscles to the brink of failure in order for them to become stronger and be able to grow in meaningful ways.

It is part of the natural world that real growth is not easy to come by. If we are lucky and well-adjusted, we might turn out to be successful, able to learn quickly, or have bodies that are easy to train. None of that compares to the ability of a person who has been through the fire and has been tested and trained and has come out on the other side stronger and fiercer and smarter and more capable than how they went in.

Righteous suffering has a purpose

All of this is to say that, at the end of the day, we are suffering. It is not a secret, though not many people admit readily how terrible life on Earth can truly be for our mortal selves. Earth is popularly known as the Planet of Sorrows among the heavenly realms. Other rungs on the ladder look down and take pity on the existence that we have to go through here. Some beings that start life on other seed planets aren't even aware of how bad it can be until they achieve the first level of Heaven and then learn that there is such a thing as the Planet of Sorrows.

Many people believe this is unfortunate. It certainly does make it hard for us to graduate out of this life, at least compared to occupants of other seed planets who can facilitate spiritual advancement with relative ease. Our difficulties stem from the root of darkness that has infected this world due to the Lucifer Rebellion, which has already been discussed. This is a sad fact of existence for us, and there is nothing that we can do to take away the reality of the hardships that we face.

That being said, because we are constantly being forced to reckon with such evil forces even in our daily existence, we also have a wildly high amount of potential that other seed planets simply do not have. Yes, this is a hard life and a difficult kindergarten to graduate out of, but for those who are able to train themselves, there is an incredibly high potential for greatness that is not as readily available to occupants of other seed planets.

Yes, there is a darkness that lingers, but there is also a great light. At the end of the day, you get what you are looking for. If you are focused on the gloom and the darkness around the world, then those shadows will ultimately consume you. Many of us have probably come across these people. Maybe they appear depressed, maybe they have lost hope, or maybe they are just a person who seems to always have negative things happening in their lives. Whatever the reason, some people are drawn toward darkness. In allowing themselves to be drawn to that chaos, they are opening themselves up to the effects of that chaos in their lives.

The difficulty is that once you allow the darkness to suck you in, it becomes extremely difficult to get out. The shadows are all around you, and it is much easier to continue to stare into the darkness because your eyes have already adjusted to it. There is, however, always the light.

Just as people who look for darkness are able to find it quickly and easily, so, too, are those who look for light in this world. By "light," we are referring to Christ, God, and the Angels. There are also some of these people that we might have encountered in our lives. Relentlessly positive and cheerful people can make us suspicious at times. We must ask the critical question of where their cheerfulness comes from.

If it is absent of knowledge or faith in Christ, then the cheerfulness is simply a mask and the person is likely looking away into the darkness of the pit. If a person is always positive, and that positivity is centered on the light that they find in Christ, then their good cheer and happiness is actually a byproduct of being transformed by a relationship with God, which has resulted in a more fulfilled spirit and higher levels of frequencies for their soul to enjoy.

The fact of the matter is that light is easier to shine and easier to see in darkness. That is what we have as an opportunity before us on Earth.

Your true treasures are in heaven

There is a parable that comes from the Philippines about a Queen who had two daughters who were both equally qualified to take over the crown after she passed away. Wanting to make sure the Queen leaves the country with the best possible ruler; she decides that she will offer a test to her daughters.

She brings them both to the great hall and her voice echoes around the huge empty cavernous space. She gives both 10 gold coins and asks them to use that money to fill the space. The first daughter goes to the market and does everything she can to buy cheap things that take up a lot of space. She uses her coins quickly and is able to buy massive amounts of what is essentially garbage. She hauls the garbage into the space and is able to fill the space without any money to spare but with every inch covered in trash.

The second daughter takes a single gold coin and goes to buy a candle from the market. When the first daughter is done, the second daughter patiently removes all the trash from the great hall and sets the candle in the middle of the great room. She lights it and the light of the candle fills the whole room.

Her mother smiles and lifts up her hand. This child has nine gold coins still left and has used her understanding and wisdom to bring about a much better and more fulfilling wholeness to the room that needed to be filled.

The truth is that our planet is filled with garbage. And many people think that they are filling the emptiness in themselves and on this planet with cheap treasures. There is, however, another way, and we have the opportunity to be like the wise daughter who uses light to drive out the darkness and to fill the room in a way that brings beauty and goodness.

Shine your light in the darkness

The light is always there, and it is up to us to determine how best to see it, how to share it, and how to let it fill the great rooms... not just in our hearts, but in the entire expanse of the world that we are a part of. It is not easy and not everyone thinks of it. In fact, most people look around and see only darkness, or if they do recognize that they are witnessing themselves to darkness, they do not always understand that the way to be properly filled is not through massive amounts of trash.

It takes a certain kind of intelligence, cleverness, and, sometimes, the right guide who can show you the way toward the light, which is always available to you. We know that the guide to be Christ and the teachings to be preserved in holy scripture. While this is an extremely difficult kindergarten class to graduate from, it is an opportunity for us to move forward through the most difficult training ground that exists among the seed planets. Think of it as the Harvard Business School of planets, because we have the opportunity to emerge as the best beings in the universe if we go through the rigorous and demanding educational system provided to us here on Earth.

There are so many metaphors throughout scripture of there being a light in the darkness that is available to us here on Earth. In Psalms 115, we read, "Thy word is a lamp for my feet, a light on my path." This stresses that the light is not only available to us but is also the way out of the darkness if we would only take the necessary steps. In John 1:5, we read the assessment of Christ that says, "The light shines in the darkness, and the darkness has not overcome it." No matter how bad the Lucifer Rebellion was, no matter how strongly Satan has dominion over our planet, it is still no match for the light that comes to us through Christ.

Other scriptures as well help to bolster this understanding—with a constant reinforcement of Christ as the light in the world—that our job is to bring the light to the world to bring glory to our Father in Heaven, and that the light is for all people, even for those shining in the darkness. Any cursory understanding of the *Holy Bible* will immediately illuminate this constant theme throughout the text.

Even the basic Sunday School children's song is meant to evoke this truth in our spiritual lives, "this little light of mine, I'm going to let it shine..." One of the first things you are taught is to *seek the light*. The more you focus on the light, the better equipped you are to be able to make the choice to have faith and trust in Christ which will offer you the next steps toward graduation from this level.

If you think about it, most of the heroes in our history are people who have symbolically been a light shining through great darkness. The trials and tribulations of this world are opportunities in disguise, presented to us by God to show how worthy we are of not just the first level of Heaven, but even the higher levels as well.

Some of the most notable examples of people who outshone their dark times include Mother Theresa, Martin Luther King Jr., and Abraham Lincoln. Each one was faced with the scourge of death and destruction wrought upon this planet by the Evil One. Each one of these eminent people, who—it should be noted—were all very close followers of Christ, were able to shine out and serve as an example of goodness not just for those in their immediate circles, but for the whole world... and stretching beyond their time into our own.

Yes, while the chaos and darkness of this world may threaten to overwhelm you, and while it does make it difficult to see the truth clearly at times, it is also a chance for our light to shine so brightly that it helps our spiritual journey go even further and deeper than it could on any another seed planet.

Lessons from our superheroes

Let's consider that one of the more popular genres of pop culture today is superheroes. It is not a surprise nor is it a coincidence that these stories resonate with the human experience/condition so much that entire movie franchises are built, and thrive, around these characters. These characters are vastly different from one another. Some have many powers, others barely have more than a good aim and lots of courage.

No matter what the case is, each superhero has a backstory or a reason why they became the person they became. Nearly every single character has a difficult journey to get to where they end up. Batman lost his parents at a young age. Captain America wasn't good enough as a boy, but became superhuman and then was frozen for decades while all his loved ones died. The Hulk couldn't control his powers which led to personal isolation and loneliness.

All these characters have amazing potential because they have gone through dark and chaotic times. Without the chaos, in fact, none of them would have become the superheroes that they needed to be.

Superman is a figure that has many Christ-like allusions in the stories, comics, and movies that focus on him as the central character. Superman was not born as Clark Kent. He is from another planet and is sent to Earth when

Krypton explodes. He not only loses his parents but also his entire home planet.

Similarly, Christ came to us not from a different place that was not this world. Christ's kingdom was not another planet, but another celestial realm altogether. Still, both Christ and Superman were not from this Earth originally; but came here to try and do good for people who were not always grateful and who were constantly fighting with one another. Christ loses so much in the Lucifer Rebellion and sees the pain of death on Earth.

This is not to endorse Superman or any superhero. This analogy is being shared to provoke the thought that these stories are so popular not because people enjoy the flash and pizzaz of superheroes, but because there is a part of each of us that recognizes the potential for greatness within each one of us, the feeling of loneliness, and the potential to shine out in bleak darkness.

This can only be done if the person embraces their powers or the Spirit of God that is within them. If Superman chose, he could have been Clark Kent the entire time. Only through willingly choosing to be Superman was he able to perform superhuman feats of strength and rescue so many people. So, too, each one of us can choose to remain humble. Life can be simple and doesn't have to present any challenges. But we have the potential to rise up above that and flourish if we unlock the faith and trust in God that is within us. Superman is not of this world, and there is a part of us that is not of this world either. If we trust that part of us, we will be able to find deeper joys in the future and beyond this world when we approach our death sleep.

The life of a Christ follower is a difficult one. It is one of trying to shine in the midst of darkness. Christ himself suffered greatly on the cross. He knew the agony and pain of human suffering and humiliation. But without his death, there could not have been any resurrection.

Simply put, we have a difficult planet to be on, but we do not have to complain about how difficult it is here. We will all know pain, suffering, and death, but we also have the potential to soar above the mundane difficulties of this world and find higher frequencies of truth and proximity to the divine. We have a unique opportunity here to rise above our limitations and show the true mettle of our faith in ways that are not an option for every being in the universe.

Most of all, we must remember that Jesus Christ came to give us a blueprint so that we may know that each of us is worthy of Heaven and eternal life. If we simply follow the path that Christ has laid before us, we will be able to fully realize our spiritual development to the highest potential ever possible.

Our real treasure

The difficulties of life on Earth make it hard for us to put God first. We have to have food and shelter, we have to work, which often takes most of each day. God, Christ, and the Angels know quite well how difficult it can be for those on Earth to break away from the daily grind because of this. These constructs of constant work and distraction from Christ are part of the system of obscurity created by Lucifer/Satan in his ruling of this earthly kingdom.

God is aware, however, and so He provides extra grace to every human. This grace is a way of understanding and patience. It does not look like God interfering with human free will. Even in the difficulties of this world, and with the Creator's grace and mercy, we are still required to take the first step and direct that step toward God and not away from Christ. Through prayer, meditation, or time with a devotional, we offer the intention to connect with Christ and become closer to God.

An enlightened being once said, "Take a single step closer to me, and I will take 10,000 steps towards you." I couldn't agree more. God desires you so badly and wants nothing more than to be in a relationship with you and see your spirit deepen, your soul thrive, your vibrations yield higher frequencies, and, ultimately, see you come to Heaven and join the heavenly body of God. All of this, though, is secondary to the truth that God gives you free will. As much as God desires all of that for you, God will not break the rules of existence to make them happen. You must take the initiative. Knowing that tomorrow is not promised, you should truly take that initiative today.

Here on Earth, we have the opportunity to accumulate spiritual gifts through good deeds and service work and through a deepening relationship with Christ, God, and the Heavens. This is our real treasure. The only treasure that matters.

PREVIEW CHAPTER FROM BOOK 1 - WELCOME TO HEAVEN. YOUR GRADUATION FROM KINDERGARTEN EARTH TO HEAVEN

Chapter 2. Does Heaven Exist?

Various allegories of Heaven can be seen in our everyday lives. From passing churches in neighborhoods whose steeples reach the sky to common expressions such as "Good heavens". Rock 'n roll can also enter our lives and give us songs that strum away to Heavenly references, such as *Knocking on Heaven's Door* by Bob Dylan, *Stairway to Heaven* by Led Zeppelin, and *Tears*

in Heaven by Eric Clapton. Indeed, Heaven can be found around many corners and blasting through radio stations. Even people who don't read the Bible know about it.

Heaven can also be that great place in the sky above the clouds, the place where all your family who passed on are waiting for you. Maybe if you are imaginative, it can be the place where you can have everything you want if you lean towards materialist tendencies and dream of these financially abundant visions of your afterlife. Whichever way you look at it, if you were to ask anyone, I'm sure they would tell you that they have heard of Heaven and that if it really does exist, they would like to go there.

The ultimate goal of any Christian faith-based being is to be in the presence of God, sit at the Father's right hand, and become one with God. The will of God wants us to know and anticipate this place so that we may think about it daily and dwell upon its glory. That's why Peter says, "According to his promise we are waiting for new heavens and a new Earth in which righteousness dwells" (*English Standard Version*, 2001,). For some, the underlying concept of being in this righteous place called Heaven is mysterious at best, and waiting for us is a lifetime goal. But let's try and figure out; what exactly is Heaven?

What is Heaven?

Our ability to imagine what the greatest place on Earth may be like, I'm sure, would be different for each person if you asked them. For example, if one were to ask ten people what their definition of a paradise is, each person would presumably have a different answer.

So what then is Heaven, and how could it be the desirable place for every person who seeks it? According to one scholar, Thomas A. Kempis, who studied scriptures and lived in the fourteenth century, believes Heaven is a place completely separate from worldly affairs and it is in seeking release from this earthly realm you will be able to set your mind on the highest form of Christ and God's Kingdom. Kempis says, "Keep yourself a stranger and a pilgrim on Earth, to whom the affairs of this world are no concern. Keep your heart free and lifted up to God, for here you have no abiding city. Daily direct your prayers and longing to Heaven, that at your death, your soul may merit to pass joyfully into the presence of God" (Kempis, 1952). From the perspective of Kempis, the "no abiding city" of Earth does not compare to the Kingdom of Heaven where the presence of God dwells and where your heart deserves to have its focus.

When you are in the Kingdom and Presence of God, all individual preferences will unify and that is what makes Heaven great. Can you even begin to imagine a being as great as He? It is not so much what Heaven is or what the place offers, but simply being in the presence of God. For any of you who have had some Divine interference in any part of life can attest to and bear witness to His greatness and eternal Love. Abiding with Him in the Kingdom of Heaven is beyond what can be compared to our earthly life.

Biblical Evidence

Throughout the Bible, there is ample evidence that supports the reality of Heaven. In Hebrew scriptures found in the Old Testament, there is some scant evidence, but it becomes clarified in New Testament Scriptures, especially through the words of Jesus himself. We will explore a few here:

The first time that the word "Heaven" appears in the *Bible* is in Genesis 1:1 "In the beginning, God created the Heaven and the earth." The first chapter of the Bible conveys to us that God's creation of Heaven happened simultaneously with God's creation of Earth. The Earth is evidently real. We live here, we see it, we interact with one another on Earth, and no one doubts the existence of this planet, so we ought to realize that this suggests the parallel statement must also be true. God created Heaven and the earth. Earth, as we know, is real, and therefore Heaven must also be.

More than that, however, by beginning with the act of creating Heaven, scripture shows us that this is the priority of God. The first thing God does in the act of creation is to make Heaven. From that starting point, the rest of the Bible orients itself between these two realms. The earthly and the temporal realm, and the eternal heavenly realm. In dozens of books of the *Bible*, there are countless references to Heaven and to God's desire for humanity to move toward attaining that very Heaven.

Psalm 115 reads as follows: "The highest Heavens belong to the LORD, but the earth He has given to man." Of course, this makes sense if we think of Earth as being removed from God. We can look around and clearly see that this is not Heaven. Therefore, knowing that Heaven was also created at the same time as Earth, we know that Heaven must be somewhere else, too. By clarifying this in the Psalms, there is the reassurance that although our scientific methods cannot locate Heaven in our understanding of the physical plane, the heavenly realm is something else entirely and just belongs to God.

John 18:36 tells us the words of Christ when he reiterates, "My kingdom is not of this world." These words are spoken in response to Pontious Pilate who has put Jesus on trial. While the Pharisees, Sadducees, and Romans are trying to trap Jesus into claiming an earthly kingdom, which would put him at odds with the Roman Empire as well as the Hebrew Temple, Jesus sidesteps their snare by clarifying that the kingdom that Jesus has dominion over is not a part of this world.

In 2 Corinthians, Paul writes about a "third Heaven" while discussing the realities of the eternal with his readers.

With this knowledge of Heaven existing outside of our earthly understanding, we can start to see a clearer picture of what Heaven is and is not. In 2 Corinthians 12:4, and in Revelations 2:7, Heaven is referred to as "Paradise." We will look into what this may mean at a later stage.

Heaven is referred to as "My Father's house" by Jesus in John 14:2, an "eternal inheritance" in 1 Peter 1:4, and is where Jesus goes to prepare a place for those who are his followers. If we are wondering who is already there, Revelation 5:11-13 tells us that there will be "thousands upon thousands, and ten thousand times ten thousand" angels occupying the heavenly realms.

Philippians 3:20-21 clarifies that true citizenship for the believers in Christ is not found on any earthly registry, but purely belongs to Heaven. Similarly, Paul shares that what is heavenly is of a purer, more enduring, substance than that which we can know on Earth.

These are several examples of biblical references to Heaven. Let's look at some of them:

- Christ calls it His "Father's house" (John 14:2)

- It is called "Paradise" (2 Corinthians 12:4, Rev 2:7)

- The "Kingdom of Heaven" (Mathew 25:1, James 2:5)

- The "Everlasting Kingdom" (2 Peter 1:11)

- A "better country", "a heavenly country" (Hebrew 11:14-16 NKJV)

- The third heaven (2 Corinthians 12:2 ESV)

- Christ said – My kingdom is not of this World (John 18:36)

- "Heaven and the highest heaven" (or "heaven and the heaven of heavens") (1 Kings 8:27, Nehemiah 9:6, Psalm 115:16)

- Paul says - They have in heaven a better and more enduring substance (Philippians 3:20-21)

- "Then I looked and heard the voice of many angels, numbering thousands upon thousands, and ten thousand times ten thousand (Revelation 5:11-13)

Deductions on Biblical Evidence

All references to Heaven that we come to read in the *Bible* are layered on top of one another. We know that they are true because we read how they complement one another and are not in contradiction. We see consistent evidence of the reality of the word of God in the *Bible* as it plays out in this earthly existence. It, therefore, only makes sense if we realize that God's Word is also the truth when it attempts to reveal the reality and nature of Heaven to us.

Heaven is a Location

What do we know from biblical evidence alone? We know that Heaven exists not as a concept of the mind, but as an actual location, a dwelling place, even if that location is beyond the scope of what we can perceive with our human senses and scientific advancements. We are also aware that the consistent references to Heaven as eternal treasure assure us that this is a place that will last forever and will be worth our efforts to finally reach it.

In the context of our imagination and as Kempis has also put it, the Earth is not our 'abiding city,' and may leave us to wonder if Heaven is just that– an abiding city in itself. If we were to attempt to define it by the context of geographical location, this reference to thinking of Heaven as a landscape is helpful because it is something relatable and that we can envision. If it is a land space and some form of geographical region like a country, it would most certainly represent all the goodness imaginable.

The reference to the Kingdom of Heaven as being some form of landscape is quoted in two different versions of the Bible in the Book of Hebrews. In the King James Version it is referred to as a "better country" (*King James Bible*, 2017/1769, Hebrews 11:14-16). In the New King James version, it is referred to as a "heavenly country" (*New King James Bible*, 1982, Hebrews 11:14-16). Understanding Heaven as being a land space provides the opportunity to embrace Heaven as a concept easily due to the comparison of our own earthly dwelling place.

While later chapters explore the concept of soul and spirit and what actually happens after we die, referred to as the *death sleep*, we can pretty much sum up here that Heaven, while perceived as a landscape, is much more than something defined by simple geographical location. But for an easily understandable reference, it may very well be an abiding city that doesn't exist on Earth yet that is described as a heavenly country.

A dwelling place of Angels

Heaven is known to be a place where angels dwell. If Heaven was just a physical space on an earthly realm, where would the multitude of angels abide with such limitations and boundaries? We all know and have heard about angels and certainly providing modern musical references for their existence may possibly be countless and would take up a lot of room in these pages. It is inferred that angels live in Heaven even though we may not actually know how many of them there are.

But, according to the Bible, there are many angels and they do exist in Heaven, not only among themselves but others as well; "then I looked and heard the voice of many angels, numbering thousands upon thousands, and ten thousand times ten thousand. They encircled the throne and the living creatures and the elders" (*New International Version*, 1973, Revelation 5:11-13). The Kingdom of Heaven must really be an astounding place that is beyond what our mortal mind can comprehend, especially if all those angels live there.

It inspires one to become humbler and understand that our personal thoughts and their constrictions limit the comprehension of our majestic imaginations that can dream about it. If it is possible to do so, we can engage in an even greater ability and envision a higher timeline and heavenly dimension where the angels dwell.

Sitting with God and Christ

The disciples of Jesus Christ were aware of the divine glory and power of being in Heaven, the Kingdom of God. They were keen on being granted a one-way ticket to eternity and some tried to do anything they could to get there.

The disciples John and James fought over who would be seated at Jesus' right hand in the Kingdom Yet to Come in two books in the Bible—the Gospels of Mark and Matthew. They approached Jesus and asked, "'Teacher,' they said, 'we want you to do for us whatever we ask.' 'What do you want me to do for you?' He asked. They replied, 'Let one of us sit at your right and the other at your left in your glory'" (*New International Version*, 1973, Mark 10:35-37). Jesus replied to them that though they are able to drink from his cup and be baptized with the holy water he is baptized with, "to sit at my right or left is not for me to grant. These places belong to those for whom they have been prepared" (*New International Version*, 1973, Mark 10:40).

According to the Gospel of Mark, this caused quite a stir among the disciples, and "when the ten heard about this, they became indignant with James and John" (*New International Version*, 1973, Mark 10:41). While there are differences in the two gospel narratives, Mark shows the disciples fighting amongst themselves, and Matthew tells of their mother intervening on their behalf and asking this favor of Jesus, "'What is it you want?' he asked. She said, 'Grant that one of these two sons of mine may sit at your right and the other at your left in your kingdom'" (*New International Version*, 1978, Matthew 20:21). The symbolism of the disciples wanting to be at the side of Jesus in the Kingdom of God in the Bible twice is significant and highlights the great value of the Kingdom of Heaven. The disciples know there is great honor and glory that comes with being at the right hand of God in the Heavenly realms.

This scenario does in fact, get them into trouble with the other disciples who are not too pleased that their peers would be having such a discussion without them. They also know the importance of being at Jesus' right hand. To be omitted from the conversation is not only insulting but upsetting to them. Jesus answers "but to sit at my right or left is not for me to grant. These places belong to those for whom they have been prepared" (*New International Version*, 1973, Mark 10:40). This message indicates that not even Christ has the jurisdiction to determine the places in Heaven.

The son of God is here to offer salvation and it is God alone who grants it. Bargaining your way into Heaven is something most people would like to believe is possible just like Christ's disciples, but we can all pretty much imagine that this is not the case and not the best way to get there.

There are many levels in Heaven

Being in God's presence is exactly what Jesus is promising to those who follow Him when He speaks the words "In my Father's house there are many dwelling-places. If it were not so, would I have told you that I go to prepare a place for you?" (*New International Version*, 1973, John 14:2).

We understand that Heaven is God's house and that there are many mansions and levels within the Heavenly realms. All of it, though, clearly belongs to Christ. Christ is the one who is the ruler of this kingdom, and we know that every kingdom has subjects, organizations, order, and structures that are overseen by the ruler. With Christ as king, we can presume, by the words he records in the gospels, what his kingdom will be (or is) like.

Jesus makes the promise that there are many dwelling places and assures His followers that this is part of His purpose for His time on Earth. He needs to tell us this so we may know what is coming next. Also, it implies what we can expect if we lead a life worthy of His Kingdom and Paradise.

If there is this grandiose construct of what a Kingdom is and what Heaven represents, why did Christ leave his Kingdom to come to Earth? While this is not entirely the scope of this book, it is sufficient to say that God and Christ desired to bring salvation to mankind. It is only through salvation that a passageway to Heaven is ensured. "I am the way, the truth, and the life. No one comes to the Father except through me" (*New International Version*, 1973, John 14:6).

At least there are 3 levels to Heaven

Based on Paul's words, we know that there are, at least, three levels of Heaven. This will be explored more fully later, but for now, it is enough to know that Heaven is complex, and the way that it is structured is beyond the basic idea of a simple realm.

Christ's kingdom is not of Earth. So where is it?

Christ said His Kingdom is not of Earth, so where is it? If we can't ask our way in like the disciples John or James tried or if we can't bargain our way in because the Bible claims that God chooses his people, what is it? What does it look like? If there is a Kingdom, it must have a lot of people in it because any definition of a Kingdom indicates that it is very large. In fact, even trying to imagine the concept of the population of Earth in this realm is truly incredible. Heaven is a Kingdom as referred to in both books of Matthew and James and more specifically, as the "Kingdom of Heaven" (*King James Bible*, 2017/1769, ;). This eternal home of God is also distinguished between the Kingdom of Heaven and the Kingdom of God.

According to the Encyclopedia of the Bible, "Mark, Luke, and John use 'the Kingdom of God' in every case, but Matthew has the form 'the Kingdom of heaven' thirty-two times and 'the Kingdom of God' only four times (Matt 12:28; 19:24; 21:31, 43)" (Encyclopedia of the Bible, (n.d)).

While the purpose of this reference is not to create an argument of semantics, it is to identify what Heaven looks like compared to what a Kingdom might actually be. In these references, a Kingdom is used interchangeably with Heaven. Accordingly, there must be a King and subjects based on the standard knowledge of what a Kingdom would be. If we consider our Father's House as the Kingdom, there must be many locations and levels that must entail a structure in place that could be cities or countries.

The Kingdom of Heaven and the Kingdom of God imply one main thing—that God is the ruler and Jesus Christ came to Earth for salvation. Some common misperceptions still permeate the atmosphere of non-believers about what Heaven really is as this chapter explores and clarifies these floating ideas.

There are enduring substances in Heaven

We know a little bit about the nature of Heaven as well, including the fact that there are an infinite number of angels in Heaven and that varying levels have different substances of purity that endure differently than anything we can conceptualize on Earth. Most importantly, though, we know that it is possible for us to become citizens of this Heaven, and that comes with many rights and a sense of belonging... only if we recognize how to get there by following Christ's words, works, and examples.

In Summary, we can make the following deductions:

- Heaven exists, Heaven is not a mind concept, it is a location, a dwelling place
- Heaven is a "better country" or a good place to look forward to
- It exists forever (everlasting kingdom)
- It is worth our effort (eternal inheritance)
- There are 3 or more levels (third heaven)
- Heaven is God's house (Father's house)
- There are many mansions or many levels in heaven
- Heaven of Heaven (indicating levels)
- Kingdom of Christ
- There are an infinite number of Angels in Heaven

Common Misperceptions

For most people, if we don't see or touch something, how can we really know it exists? Our minds like to fool us into thinking that things are real only if we use our physical senses. Without imagination how would we really understand and know any difference? When it comes to believing in God and knowing Our Father and Heaven, are they really as present as we are supposed to believe? While there can certainly be many doubts, there can be a few good reasons for this.

If we have never seen it, how are we supposed to believe in it? Why should anything that incredible really exist for us and if it does exist, why isn't it here on Earth? While our mind can try and convince us about all the reasons why Heaven shouldn't exist, believing in the reasons could just be a page turn away from fueling our faith. If we can change the mundane stories, we like to tell ourselves we may be able to open-up to the sacred perceptions that are waiting to be experienced. Perhaps even more miracles would really happen rather than believing that they don't exist at all.

Misperception: Heaven is one single place

The first common misperception to assess is the belief that Heaven is a single place where only angels live. While we hear so much about angels, have we ever wondered where else they would live? How can humans dwell in the same place as angels?

In the book of Revelations, it describes Heaven as having many angels but also other living creatures and elders: "then I looked and heard the voice of many angels around the throne, and also of the living creatures and of the elders. Their number was countless thousands, plus thousands of thousands" (*Christian Standard Bible*, 2001, Revelation 5:11). While angels and other creatures can intermingle past the pearly gates, there is reason to support that it is a grand place filled with many creatures and a Kingdom, not of this Earth, as it further says in the Bible when "Jesus answered, My kingdom is not of this world: if my kingdom were of this world, then would my servants fight, that I should not be delivered to the Jews: but now is my kingdom not from hence" (*King James Bible*, 2017/1769, John 18:36). Heaven indeed is a place where more than just angels dwell, it is a Kingdom set apart from this world where many beings live together.

Misperception – Living in Heaven with a physical body

Knowing that Heaven is a place where people dwell among angels, it would therefore not be hard to assume that when we enter Heaven, we will live without a body. This is based on the idea that once we die and go to Heaven, we will be formless. To some people, this may sound appealing whereas for others, it sounds mind-boggling.

How can we live or exist without a body? If one has had low self-esteem issues or felt disconnected from the beauty and glory of their earthly vessel, being formless may just be what some people want and come as a relief. It means you finally don't have to worry about those weight-loss diets you have always been planning whether in this life or the next.

However, the idea of separation from our bodies and the possible consequence of the loss of identity can be a daunting concept because it is quite simply difficult to imagine living without it. The feeling of being formless is not desirable when knowing that if it is possible to retain the vessel we are familiar with, it will be better.

When death is at our doorstep or if we have a fear of death, keeping our body and identity just the way it is can feel like the familiar route and the safer, more predictable option. According to the following scripture, the formlessness some fear is not even true, "for we know that if the earthly tent we live in is destroyed, we have a building from God, an eternal house in heaven, not built by human hands" (*New International Version*, 1973, 2 Corinthians 5:1).

The fact that we aren't beings just floating around in space may offer some solace to those who find the idea of disembodiment frightful. According to this scripture, we are given new bodies that will house our identity, soul, and spirit (to be discussed in later chapters). How you perceive the afterlife, with bodies intact or by the design of God's own hands will come to fruition, and in ways that only God knows.

Misperception – Heaven is a boring place

Knowing that we have a form or some vessel as we enter the Kingdom of the Almighty, what exactly is it that we do there? Since we are all earth-bound beings, most of us can say we like the idea of a playground on earth. We know that there are things to do, lots to see, and places to go. The misconception is that when we go to Heaven, even though all is good and well there and it sounds nice, *what exactly is there to do?*

Can we really just sit around listening to harps all day and gaze upon the heavenly clouds with compliant acceptance? When you come into a relationship with God and know that he is the Creator of Heaven and Earth, then quite realistically you will understand that he is not boring. In fact, quite the opposite. God is infinite, and so is His creation. God has created our laughter, our funny bones, the adrenaline in our bodies, our taste buds, sensory experiences, and the excitement and passion for life that exists in the Heavens.

In fact, to believe anything otherwise furthers the mission of dark forces that would prefer to have you be under the impression that this place does not exist. This notion is supported in Revelations where it says that "no longer will there be any curse. The throne of God and of the Lamb will be in the city, and his servants will serve him" (*New International Version*, 1973,). The children of God will enter the holy city and no negative curse can stop them. Moreover, there is plenty to do in the Kingdom of God, just as there has been on Earth. Perhaps even more than this earthly realm can even imagine. In this place you will also eat, drink, and be merry as you do now and as will be done in eternal life. "Whether you eat or drink, or whatever you do, do all to the glory of God" (*New International Version*, 1973, 1 Corinthians, 10:31). Only the limit of our imaginations places restrictions and the idea of boredom in Paradise Kingdom created by God.

Misperception – Everything is perfect in Heaven, nothing to do

Aside from the interesting and stimulating life that awaits us, we know that Heaven is not simply a place where nothing bad happens or where everything is perfect all the time. The spiritual ecstasy that is in store for those who dwell in the house of the Lord and to sit in His presence is unfathomable to our earth-based existence and limited ability to sense and understand. The book of Romans declares, "for I consider that the sufferings of this present time are not worthy to be compared with the glory which shall be revealed in us. For the earnest expectation of the creation eagerly waits for the revealing of the sons of God" (*New International Version*, 1973, Romans 8:18/19).

The spiritual riches offered in this divine place truly appeal to earthly beings and can elevate our existence beyond our current imaginings. Not only does the promise of Heaven offer us peace and entertainment in the afterlife but, if we can truly envision such a place of righteousness and spiritual salvation, then our own present Internal Kingdom within us will be at peace and rest here on Earth before we even get there.

So, where is Heaven?

Most of us live a fast-paced life in modern society. The convenience of GPS can take us to where we want to go almost instantly and everything we want to know can be accessed by our fingertips. All GPS involves is an address and when you set the location, you not only know how to find it but also how to get there.

When it comes to knowing where Heaven is, if it is neither in our neighborhood nor within a one-hundred-mile radius, is it even worth going? It might as well be as far away as Timbuktu, right? That is why when we begin to connect with our inner Kingdom within, we don't have to look for or follow an external map to the Kingdom of God. We can close our eyes and connect with our living breath, and the gentle, comforting presence of God the Father Himself can be with us at any time and anywhere.

GPS of Heaven is Frequencies and Vibrations

Imagine you have a GPS that can transport you to places by tuning your frequencies or vibrations. Setting your GPS to say 4th dimension (as opposed to 3rd dim of Earth), the GPS will transport you to some space and time continuum. What does life look like? Does life exist in this time-space? What is the reality in this frequency space?

Modern-day physics is just starting to explore the infiniteness of the time-space continuum. String theory is gaining popularity and is but one theory that sheds some light on this fascinating subject. "According to string theory, absolutely everything in the universe—all of the particles that make up matter and forces—is comprised of tiny vibrating fundamental strings".

There are many experiments conducted by the US Military by manipulating localized vibrations, which resulted in the disappearance of Navy ships (The Montauk Project). It is beyond the scope of this book to talk about these experiments; however, it is important to know that within the realm of possibility, there exists a time-space continuum that is beyond our current knowledge and understanding.

Worlds of Heaven have a frequency and vibration to them. As you evolve spiritually, when your frequency and vibrational patterns match that of the heavenly world, you will be granted entrance to that Heavenly world. This is how evolution happens. When you understand Heaven, its structure, and its different levels, you will realize that Creation and the Universe operate in precision under God's guiding hand.

Our Journey begins

Though Heaven waits for our arrival, the passing of our mortal lives on this earthly plane makes the waiting worth it because the righteousness of God can be felt in our daily lives until we get there.

It's worth noting that just because we have begun our journey into the Heavenly Realm, this does not mean we have already become one with the presence of God. If we reduced the entire journey to a single step, we would be underestimating the complexity and magnitude of God's great Design of all that is and ever will be. Your own evolutionary journey in your relationship with God represents your depth and experience of the eternal Kingdom from within and most certainly in the afterlife.

As we continue to understand the journey and exploration of Heaven and all that it mightily entail, how can we exactly be sure that we are indeed on the way there? What part of our lives and personal development ensures that we will be guaranteed a ticket to this luminous place at the end of our mortal life?

The next chapter explores these questions and more, including which path we should take to ensure our arrival after our mortal life lands us at these pearly gates of glory.

Welcome to Heaven. Your Graduation from Kindergarten Earth to Heaven

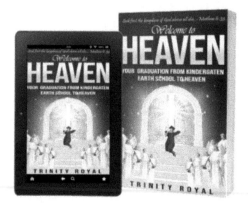

Scan Me

"I go and prepare a place for you, I will come back and take you to be with me that you also may be where I am." - John 14:3

Ever wonder **if Heaven is real**? What **proof** do we have?

How does one **go to Heaven**? What are the **minimum requirements for Heaven**?

Why **Life of Earth is your Kindergarten school**?

Trinity explores the following:

- Isn't Heaven **just a mind concept**? What is the proof of its existence? Why do I even bother about Heaven? What is in it for me?

- What are the **minimum requirements to go to Heaven or the ticket booth to Heaven**?

- Why is life on Earth your **kindergarten school**?

- Are there **different levels to heaven? If so, how many? What are they?** Does the **time and space continuum exist in Heaven?** If so how different is it compared to Earth's time and space?

SOS - *Save yOur Soul*

Scan Me

"For what shall it profit a man, if he shall gain the whole world, and lose his own soul?" - *Mark* 8:36

Ever Wonder **What Happens After You Die**? Is it the end?

What did **Christ** Say about death and life after mortal death?

Is there a way to Save yOur Soul? If so How?

What exactly is **Soul** and **Spirit**, is it just a new age concept? What did Christ Say?

Trinity considered to be one of the bridges between Heaven and Earth, shares general Angelic knowledge. This book explores:

What are the unseen parts of us that make us who we are? What is left behind after Mortal death and what happens to these **unseen parts of us**?

What exactly is **Soul** and **Spirit**, is it just a new age concept? What did Christ Say? Is there a way to Save yOur Soul? If so How? Does Heaven actually exist? Can a ticket to Heaven be guaranteed?

Lucifer Rebellion. Christ vs. Satan – Final Battle for Earth Has Begun

Scan Me

Multiple Award-winning Book

"extraordinary book" "Definitely a five-star read" - [International Review of Books]

Ever wonder **why there is a War between GOD and the Devil?** Ever wonder how the **War in Heaven started or what the Lucifer Rebellion is**?

Ever wonder why War in heaven came to Earth or why darkness still exists on Earth? And why did God send Christ to Earth?

This book explores:

- How and Why did the **war in Heaven start**? How did the War in Heaven come to Earth?

- Why did **God send Christ** to planet Earth? Was it to save Humanity and the Universe?

- What exactly happened during **Christ's First Coming** event? What is expected during the Second Coming event?

Trinity takes us on a **journey beyond time and space** to find the answers to these questions that every believer should know.

Lucifer Rebellion. Christ vs Satan – The Second Coming of Christ

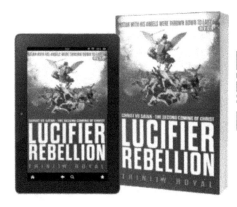

Ever wonder **why there is a War between GOD and Devil?**

Ever wonder how the **War in Heaven started or what Lucifer Rebellion is**? **and why War in Heaven came to Earth** and why darkness still exists on Earth?

This book explores:

- How and Why did the **war in Heaven start**?

- How did the War in Heaven come to Earth?

- Why did **God send Christ** to planet Earth? Was it to save Humanity and the Universe?

- What are the effects of War on Earth and in Heaven?

- What exactly happened during **Christ's First Coming** event?

- What is expected during the Second Coming event?

I invite you to join me on a journey beyond space and time when the Lucifer Rebellion started and the reasons for Christ's First and Second Coming events.

Christ & Demons - Unseen Realms of Darkness

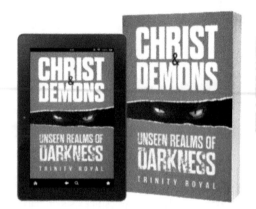

"The reason the Son of God appeared was to destroy the Devil's work." -*Ephesians 6:12*

Is there an **UNSEEN world of Darkness** hidden in front of our eyes?

Ever wonder why **Evil** exists on Earth? Ever wonder how **Satan got to planet Earth a**nd what exactly is the Dark Empire Agenda?

Ever wonder why Christ chose planet Earth for His great Bestowal?

What is the **agenda of Darkness**? Why do God and Christ let dark forces flourish on Earth? Does God have a plan? What is it?

What are the differences between **Demons, Evil Spirits, and Ghosts**? How does **Selling one's Soul to the devil** happen?

Son of Man becomes Son of God. One Event that Changed the History of the World

Award-Winning Book

"*an opportunity for the reader to embark on a journey with Him, feel what He feels*"

"*A fascinating description and story of how Christ emerged, changed and developed into the highest of holiest beings, second only to God.*"

"*An exceptional and well-written novel without the preaching and pointless prose and verbiage of others of this type*"

There is **ONE event** that is the true turning point in the history of Earth. This is not the Birth or Baptism of Jesus, but it is the **fight with the Devil**

Ever wonder what would have happened to Earth if Christ failed against Satan? This was a real possibility, although it is considered blasphemous to talk about it.

From Suffering to Healing

Scan Me

"I highly recommend this for anyone *who has ever suffered in their lives*, and, in all honesty, who hasn't?"

Why do **bad things happen to good people**?

Why does your **Life journey lead you to suffer?**

The Answer is to Heal You.

Your suffering is the epitome of a **blessing in disguise.** Wrapped in darkness and suffering, it removes the ground from beneath your feet and leaves you fearful, fragile, and devoid of meaning in life.

Most beings that we adore or worship have gone through dark times in their life. This includes Christ, Buddha, Gandhi, Nelson Mandela, Oprah, Abraham Lincoln, etc. This process is necessary as it redefines a person, re-makes one character, and chips away the darkness to bring out the luster of your **Real Self.** This is your **METAMORPHOSIS.**

Dark Night of the Soul

<u>Award-Winning Book</u>

Our wounds are often the openings into the best and the most beautiful parts of us." -David Richo

Ever wonder **why suffering happens for no known reason...**

Ever wonder **why your Soul is longing**...

Have you ever felt like you have a **splinter in your mind, that does not let you off the hook..**

If so, <u>**you are chosen for a purpose. There is GOD's hand working in your life.**</u>

While there are many reasons people suffer (most are self-made or bad decisions or external in nature); the type of Suffering referred to as the "Dark Night
of the Soul" has a clear and definite purpose. **The purpose is your Soul's growth.**

<u>**Your Answers and Healing await. Click on Buy Now.**</u>

What Happened on Easter Saturday? 36 hr mystery between Death and Resurrection

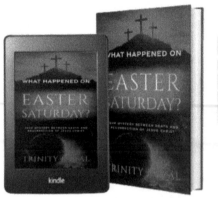

"A five-star read, absolutely."

"It stands to reason that Saturday was a critical time for Him"

"I highly recommend this incredible book as it takes the reader through both the physical and spiritual journey of Him as he underwent His transformation. **A five-star read, absolutely.**"

"I for one never really thought about that Saturday, so for me **it was a riveting experience**, learning about that previously overlooked time."

Ever wonder **what happened when Christ was inside the Tomb for 36 hrs** between death and resurrection?

Ever wonder **what body did Christ have after Resurrection**? and why the **resurrection process take 3 days?** why not 1-day or 2-days?

Free books to our readers

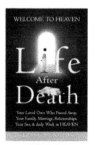

War in Heaven came to Earth. Satan Rebellion:

https://dl.bookfunnel.com/ea12ys3dmk

Your Life in Heaven:

https://dl.bookfunnel.com/vg451qpuzs

References

King James Bible. (2017). King James Bible Online. (Original work published 1769)

Georgiou, Aristos. (August, 2022). Most People Who Have Near Death Experiences Report the Same Things After. Newsweek.

God of Light and Love. (n.d.). What's After Life?

Will We Recognize and Be Reunited With Our Loved Ones in Heaven. (n.d). Grace To You.<>

Will We Know Our Loved Ones in Heaven? (n.d). Bible Study. >

Thomas Moore Quotes. (n.d.). *Thomas Moore Quotes*. BrainyQuote.

https://truthbook.com/

About Author

Trinity is a multi-award-winning author and a spiritual warrior. While life might not always work out according to plan, Trinity was able to take valuable lessons from each new experience. Trinity grew and developed and now shares a passion for enlightening others on spiritual knowledge in the hopes of closing the gap between Heaven and Earth. Trinity's writings reflect the depths of a passion and desire to connect with everyone seeking spiritual growth and education.

You can learn more at www.RocketshipPath2God.com or @ https://www.facebook.com/TrinityRoyalBooks

Milton Keynes UK
Ingram Content Group UK Ltd.
UKHW020733161023
430697UK00016B/726